The Celtic Trail

The Official Guide to National Cycle Network
Routes 4 and 47 from Fishguard to Chepstow

YMUNWCH Â'R MUDIAD

sustrans

JOIN THE MOVEMENT

The author and publisher have made every effort to ensure that the information in this publication is accurate, and accept no responsibility whatsoever for any loss, injury or inconvenience experienced by any person or persons whilst using this book.

published by
pocket mountains ltd
6 Church Wynd, Bo'ness EH51 0AN
pocketmountains.com

ISBN-13: 978-0-9554548-6-8

Text and photography copyright © Pocket Mountains Ltd and Sustrans 2008 except images on pages 25, 52 and 87 courtesy Colin Palmer (www.buyimage.co.uk)

Format and design © Pocket Mountains Ltd 2008

A catalogue record for this book is available from the British Library

All route maps are based on 1945 Popular Edition Ordnance Survey material and revised from field surveys by Pocket Mountains Ltd, 2008. © Pocket Mountains Ltd and Sustrans 2008

All rights reserved. No part of this publication may be reproduced, stored in a retrieval system, or transmitted in any form or by any means, electronic or mechanical, including photocopying and recording, unless expressly permitted by Pocket Mountains Ltd and Sustrans.

Printed in Poland

Introduction

Rich in history, diverse in landscape, strong in character, Wales (or Cymru to its own people) is a perfectly formed realm with the power of a spell. I wonder if there is another country in the world better suited to a long-distance bike ride.

The Celtic Trail stretches across the entire breadth of South Wales, from the Atlantic Ocean to the English border, taking in the raw and romantic Pembrokeshire coast, the forgotten rural hinterland of Carmarthenshire and the famous 'Valleys' that powered the Industrial Revolution. Following quiet (sometimes completely silent) rural lanes, traffic-free paths and dedicated cycleways, the route takes in many of the most interesting historical and contemporary features Wales has, from ancient megaliths to the spectacular single-span greenhouse at the National Botanic Garden of Wales, via Roman roads, a chain of medieval fortresses, dismantled railways and the ruins of mighty ironworks.

In particular, the Celtic Trail makes great use of the once neglected highways of the Industrial Revolution, following arrow-straight tramroads and canal towpaths that formerly bore iron ore and coal down from the valleys to the coast, and crossing parks on the sites of Victorian mines and steel mills that have recently been returned to nature. By merely pedalling through these places, you are part of the regeneration process.

The Celtic Trail is made up principally of Route 4, a linear trail of 359km (223 miles) from Fishguard to Chepstow that broadly follows the south coast. Many cyclists will relish the opportunity of completing this epic ride in one run. There are, however, four alternative sections that veer inland, often through more remote and mountainous countryside, and rejoin the principal route later. These alternative sections are in no way inferior – in fact, they cross landscapes that might be even more glorious – and they go under the collective name of Route 47. Thus the Celtic Trail provides a myriad of options: firstly, anyone riding Route 4 can simply veer away from the coast for a section of Route 47 and then return to Route 4. These alternatives also offer four circular rides ranging from two to seven days; and if that's not enough options, there are also three figure of eight rides, taking in two loops each, centred on Carmarthen, Swansea and Pontypridd. This guide points out the most obvious loops, with suggestions

On Swansea seafront ▶

about the best direction to ride them: obviously, if you do the loops, you'll have to read some of the route descriptions in reverse.

To marry with the Sustrans Celtic Trail East and West maps (available from sustrans.org.uk), and to a lesser extent to highlight the difference in topography, this guide breaks the Celtic Trail into two, at the "ugly, lovely town" (as Dylan Thomas put it) of Swansea, Wales' second city. To the west, Route 4 jags out into the Atlantic to reach St Davids Head, the Welsh Land's End, before curling round St Brides Bay and wriggling along the south coast, occasionally snaking inland to cross the great estuaries that drain all that rain back into the ocean. Route 47 writhes up and down the Preseli Hills, and follows a wonderful section of dismantled railway to Llanelli. To the east of Swansea, Route 47 climbs 600m into the forests above Neath, following a Roman track over the mountains, across the mighty Rhondda Valley and down to Pontypridd, before veering north again through the industrial heartland that created modern Wales, to rejoin Route 4 in Newport. Meanwhile, Route 4 skirts round Swansea Bay and heads over the foothills of the same fabled

Valleys before crossing the Gwent Levels to reach Chepstow.

Of course, Chepstow may not mark the end of your journey: if you're following Route 4 to London, for example, the mighty castle here might just be the end of the beginning. This medieval town on the English border has been a crossroads for centuries, and a lattice of inspiring Sustrans routes lead off in every direction.

Finding your way

As with the best Sustrans routes, the Celtic Trail follows a fine blend of purpose-built cyclepaths, shared-use paths, quiet minor roads and traffic-free sections. There are a few short sections on busier roads where due care must be taken. Traffic-free sections are suitable for all bikes, with the exception of racers, but a hybrid touring or cyclo-cross bike is recommended for those intending to follow the route in full. More testing off-road sections are highlighted, where a pannier-laden rider will find their progress slowed, and for Section 12 (Swansea to Pontypridd on Route 47) a mountain bike is recommended.

Generally speaking, the route is very well signposted with the blue National Route 4 and 47 signs. These are carefully sited to give the cyclist advance notice of changes in direction: you quickly become adept at

spotting them. In places, these are augmented by smaller Route 4 and 47 stickers and occasionally, where following the route is very tricky, by a yellow bicycle painted on the tarmac. Be aware that signs can go missing: follow them in conjunction with the latest Sustrans maps and you shouldn't have a problem. In common with the entire National Cycle Network, the Celtic Trail is under constant improvement so bear in mind that in places it may be at variance with the map. If there is a disparity, follow the signs, which will direct you onto the newest route section.

A number of sections are through parks and along dismantled railway lines and there's even a stretch following the Pembrokeshire Coast Path National Trail: please be aware of pedestrians and dog walkers who share the route, and act courteously towards them at all times. In urban areas, cyclists should apply the same streetwise principles they would when travelling through unfamiliar cities on foot. Be aware of your surroundings, especially if travelling alone, and preferably time your journey so you travel during daylight.

Sustrans volunteer rangers monitor the entire route, ensuring it is signposted and maintained. If you do encounter any difficulty, please do contact Sustrans Cymru, the local authority, or the police if necessary.

The National Cycle Network and Sustrans in Wales

Sustrans is the UK's leading sustainable transport charity, working on practical projects so people can choose to travel in ways that benefit their health and the environment. The charity is behind many groundbreaking projects, including the National Cycle Network, and works with the public, local authorities, employers and schools. By 2007, the Network had expanded to comprise 19,312km (12,000 miles) of predominantly traffic-free trails,

traffic-calmed roads and quiet lanes. A third of the entire Network is traffic-free: the remainder follows quiet minor roads where possible. The expansion of the Network continues apace for the benefit of cyclists, walkers and others, extending the length and breadth of the UK and linking most of its main towns and cities.

In Wales, the Sustrans story is also gathering pace. The Celtic Trail is one of two major routes – the other is National Route 8 (Lôn Las Cymru, from Holyhead to Cardiff or Chepstow) – which extend the length or breadth of the country. Many smaller routes spin off these arteries like the intricate pattern of a Celtic knot. Other major routes include Route 81 (Lôn Cambria, which crosses the heart of Wales from Aberystwyth to Shrewsbury), Route 82 (Aberystwyth to Fishguard, connecting with the Celtic Trail) and the well-known Route 8 (the Taff Trail, which the Celtic Trail briefly follows). The Sustrans website has details on all routes in Wales and it's a useful tool for keeping abreast of developments and improvements on all existing routes.

Using this guide

This guidebook is for daytrippers, weekenders and families looking for short cycles that make the most of the dismantled railway lines and regeneration parks that South Wales has in abundance, just as much as it's aimed at anyone who plans to follow the Celtic Trail from start to finish. The average day section is a comfortable 36km or so, though sections do vary in length depending on the terrain and suitable stopping points.

Timings given at the start of each section are roughly based on an average flat speed of 15km/h, with additional time built in for uneven terrain and ascent. These timings are only a guide: be aware that you could find yourself behind time or, conversely, able to complete several sections in a day.

The book describes riding the Celtic Trail

◄ By the Fourteen Locks Canal Centre

from west to east: there's one good reason for this – the prevailing southwesterly winds. Section 1 is unavoidably into it, but from then on, the wind is with you and if you ride the whole route, you'll almost certainly feel it pressing gently on your back at some stage. Suggestions have also been made regarding which way round to ride the various excellent loops that use Routes 4 and 47, often with the wind in mind.

Stopping points have been chosen with regard to a combination of things including railway access, tourist attractions and places to stay. The Celtic Trail is about more than the cycling, and that is where the overnights really come into their own. If you know Wales well, you'll see it with new eyes on the Celtic Trail; if it's your first time, evidence of almost the entire history of this fascinating country lies alongside or just off this route. It's worth taking time, even whole days, off the bike to explore the medieval towns and castle ruins, stroll along the beaches and digest the industrial heritage. You'll find highlighted in this book some of the more interesting places to visit, but these are just the start.

When to go and what to take

Wales' reputation for rain is exaggerated. That said, the prevailing weather in the British Isles does comes from the west making Wales the disembarkation point for much that the Atlantic throws at us: this includes plenty of precipitation and if you ride the Celtic Trail from end to end, you'll certainly get wet at some point. The driest and sunniest months are May to August and this is the safest period to attempt the ride. But you can also strike it lucky in April – in 2007, it was hotter than July – whilst September and October can throw up an interesting variety of rambunctious weather, from big Atlantic storms thumping Pembrokeshire to periods of sustained high pressure. Campsites, hostels and hotels will usually be open in these months but quieter. There is also less tourist traffic on the roads.

Wales has a temperate climate: it's rarely too hot or too cold. While good wet weather gear is essential at any time of year, you don't need to carry too many layers. A checklist of recommended clothing would also include gloves, overshoes, light but warm and quick-drying layers, padded shorts, a helmet, sunglasses and, if you're going to be riding at dusk, reflective clothing.

On a hot day, sunscreen is vital, especially in the west where the wind can mask the power of the sun. It goes without saying that you should take plenty of water, particularly on the long, remote sections where supply is intermittent at best. A bell is very handy in built-up areas and on shared-use paths where there are lots of walkers. Also take lights: even if you don't intend to cycle at night, it's good to know you have them. Always, without fail, carry a pump, spare tubes, tyre levers and a basic tool kit – there are entire sections of the

Reaching the route

The Celtic Trail is very well served by rail links – there are 17 stations on or near the route – and understandably, most cyclists use the train to start and finish their journey. Though Fishguard Harbour (the start point) only has one train a day (and one nightly), most of these stations have more regular services. For anyone riding short linear sections or loops on the Celtic Trail, using the railway is very convenient.

Arriva Trains Wales is the main train provider in Wales. All services along the Celtic Trail have the capacity to carry bikes, for free, but it's often limited to two. Some routes require reservations, while on others space is allocated on a first come, first served basis. There are also restrictions on bicycles on the Valleys and Cardiff Local Routes during peak hours (07.30 – 09.30 and 16.00 – 18.00). It's not nearly as complicated as it sounds though, and reservations are free, so it's always worth booking in advance if you can (0870 9000 773 /arrivatrainswales.co.uk).

First Great Western also operate trains between Newport and Swansea – there are six dedicated spaces, bikes are carried for free and again, it's advisable to make reservations (08457 000 125 /firstgreatwestern.co.uk).

Unfortunately, there are no cycle-friendly bus services that operate along the Celtic Trail.

Celtic Trail without bike shops, so you need to be able to carry out basic roadside repairs. With this in mind, get your bike serviced before you go.

Finally, although the sketch maps in this guide offer sufficient navigation, it's well worth taking the two dedicated Sustrans maps – Celtic Trail West and East – with you. In common with all Sustrans maps, these detail the route surface, cumulative distance in mile increments, steep sections and railway stations, as well as highlighting points of interest and places where the route is harder to follow.

Where to stay

In each section, you'll find brief information on the accommodation available at the end of the relevant route stage. This list is by no means exhaustive: it highlights budget options such as campsites and hostels, with particular attention given to more unusual, interesting and, of course, cycle-friendly choices. For a complete list of places to stay which subscribe to the Cyclists Welcome scheme overseen by VisitWales, go to cycling.visitwales.com or Freephone 08701 211251.

Cycling with children

Cycling is a brilliant way for the whole family to get out and enjoy the countryside, fresh air and exercise. Many sections of the Celtic Trail are suitable as shorter trips for families, and cycle hire – often with child helmets and baby seats – is available at bike shops along the way: advanced booking is recommended.

If you're new to cycling with kids, some common sense is all you need to ensure your outing is both safe and fun:

● Don't overestimate what your child is capable of. Even small hills really sap a child's energy, especially those under eight years old. Bring plenty of fun snacks and drinks to keep their spirits up.

● Study the route beforehand: this book advises which sections of the Celtic Trail are family friendly. Naturally, the safest route is one away from traffic. Where on-road family-friendly sections are advised, it is assumed children will be supervised at all times. If there is only one adult, you should ideally cycle behind your child and wear reflective clothing.

● Children should always wear a securely fitted helmet, whether they are being carried on your bike or riding their own. Check before your trip whether it still fits and is in good condition.

● Like helmets, bikes can soon be outgrown: it is dangerous for a child to ride a bike that is too big or small.

● From around 6-9 months, when babies can support their heads well, they can travel with you on a well-fitted bike seat or trailer. It's important to be aware how a baby seat affects your bike handling, especially dismounting, and that babies will be unprepared for bumps, making uneven off-road trails less suitable. Do consider, as well, that they aren't moving and will be affected by the wind, so even in good weather make sure they are well wrapped up.

West: Fishguard to Swansea

From the ocean, Celtic Trail West follows coastal trails and crosses remote, ancient landscapes that bear all the hallmarks of the Celtic Fringe: unkempt, whitewashed farmsteads sunk into the hillsides, sandy coves and lichen-covered cliffs, sod hedges sprouting vivid yellow, coconut-scented gorse, antique stone walls and stunted wind-bent trees.

You have to make your first major route decision on the Celtic Trail almost immediately: Routes 4 and 47 split just outside Fishguard. Route 47 heads east along the Gwaun Valley, Europe's oldest glacial vale, and up onto the wild heights of the Preseli Hills. There are standing stones, tumuli, cairns, cromlechs and burial chambers galore, and you pedal beneath the weathered tors of Carn Menyn, where the 'bluestones' of Stonehenge originated. After the small town of Crymych, the route rises and falls innumerable times to cross the small but powerful streams that drain into the great rivers and estuaries of West Wales.

Route 4 heads southwest from Fishguard to reach St Davids Head, the Welsh Land's End. The romance of this stretch of Atlantic coast, with its coves, sea stacks and pretty cottages, is unmistakable. St Davids Cathedral, one of medieval Europe's great pilgrimage sites, is a must-see and, if the weather is fair as you cycle round the fine sweep of St Brides Bay, the glorious beaches will be difficult to resist. A lovely traffic-free section – ideal for kids – including the final stretch of Brunel's remarkable engineering project, the Great Western Railway, connects the county town of Haverfordwest with Neyland.

South of the Cleddau Estuary, you pass Pembroke Castle, an awesome fist of limestone and one of the major seats of power in Welsh history, and the unspoilt, pastel-painted seaside town of Tenby. Route 4 leaves the coast and takes to the hills of Carmarthenshire on timeless rural lanes, heading inland via the picturesque town of Laugharne, formerly home to

POWERED → BY VEG OIL

GOODWICK

the great Welsh bard, Dylan Thomas. Routes 4 and 47 meet and split again in Carmarthen, where there are good rail links.

Now Route 4 heads south along the Towy Estuary via Kidwelly, still dominated by its Norman castle, and the scented pines of Pembrey Forest, to reach the Millennium Coastal Park – an outstanding regeneration project that hugs the Burry Estuary for more than 20km. This is the most family-friendly section of the entire Celtic Trail and is serviced by several railway stations. Once over the River Loughor, there's a gentle descent through the Clyne Valley – again, good for kids – to Swansea.

Route 47 continues east from Carmarthen,

along the Towy Valley to reach the National Botanic Garden of Wales, before heading south out of the hills. There's a wonderful section of traffic-free cyclepath, faintly downhill on a dismantled railway line, from Cefneithin to Llanelli, where the two routes rejoin.

The entire western section of the Celtic Trail provides several options: a tour of Pembrokeshire, from Carmarthen to Fishguard via the Preseli Hills and back via Haverfordwest and Tenby is one; a loop via the National Botanic Garden, Llanelli and Kidwelly is another. Of course, they can be combined to make an excellent 225km figure of eight.

Fishguard to St Davids

Distance 31km/19.5 miles (2km traffic-free) **Terrain** One long ascent out of Fishguard, then undulating along the coast with a few sharp but brief climbs; mainly minor roads with a short section of cyclepath and an even shorter stretch of A-road. No family-friendly sections
Time 3-4 hours **Ascent** 390m

A glorious day on the edge, following the craggy Pembrokeshire coast from Fishguard to St Davids Head, the Welsh Land's End. Make time to paddle, swim or picnic at one of the beaches or coves before arriving at the smallest cathedral city in the UK. If the prevailing southwesterly wind is blowing hard, it's a tougher ride than you imagine.

The ride starts beside the Irish Sea at Ocean Lab (tourist information centre and café), the modern building on Goodwick Harbour. From the railway station and the Fishguard-Rosslare ferry terminal, follow the road inland with the cliffs on your right, past the ferry office to the roundabout: Ocean Lab is in front of you. Pick up the cyclepath here, along the front, heading away from the terminals and uphill beside the A40. The cyclepath leaves the main road, crosses a minor road and climbs again through a clump of pine trees to a junction where Routes 47 and 4 split for the first time: left towards Carmarthen via the Preseli Hills (see page 34), right to St Davids.

Goodwick Harbour is the modern, functional part of Fishguard. The old or

'Lower' harbour lies back towards the sea (follow Route 47). It's worth a visit if you can suppress your desire to get the journey underway. The glitzy 1971 version of *Under Milk Wood* starring Richard Burton and Elizabeth Taylor was filmed around this picturesque port at the mouth of the River Gwaun.

Route 4 follows a cyclepath alongside the A40, ducking under it, before taking a lane off to the right towards Manorowen. You join the A487 for 1km, taking a right down another quiet lane, again climbing towards Ffynnon Druidion, the highest point of the ride today. If you haven't yet encountered the wind, the stunted trees, bent like old men over their sticks, proclaim the prevailing direction.

The route dashes into and scrambles out of two small, heavily-wooded valleys (Tregwynt – a working woollen mill with a café – is at the bottom of one) before turning right at a crossroads. A swift, winding descent ends in Abercastle – a classic west coast cove with pretty cottages tucked into the hill above the harbour. The disused limekilns – a feature of many ports on the Pembrokeshire coastline – and the empty warehouses are legacies of a time when Abercastle heaved with trade.

It's a steep climb out of Abercastle. Near the top, take the first farm track on the right for a five-minute detour to Carreg Samson, a fine example of a megalithic cromlech. There are many prehistoric sites in West Wales but Carreg Samson – six squat standing stones with a hefty capstone, hunkered down in a field overlooking the Irish Sea – seems immaculately fashioned for the landscape.

If you find prehistory a little dry, there are refreshments in the next village, Trefin (Ship Inn, Oriel-y-Felin Gallery and Tearoom). Some 2km further on, via a short detour – turn right at the crossroads in Llanrhian – is the gloriously-situated Sloop Inn at Porthgain. Here again, the remnants of small-scale industry recall the age when Pembrokeshire granite and slate were exported across Britain.

Route 4 rolls gently towards St Davids Head, through treeless heathland and fields divided by sod banks and stone walls running mesh-like down to the cliffs and sea stacks. There are fine views over St George's Channel – often illuminated by patches of fitful sunshine – and fleeting glimpses of the purple-grey stonework of the cathedral, seemingly embedded in the ground. At the crossroads with the B4583, you can turn right for a 1km detour to the magnificent but often crowded beach at Whitesands or continue on the route down a steep hill to the cathedral complex, built for safety's sake in the hollow of the Alun Valley, out of sight of ships of marauding pagans off the coast. St David, Dewi Sant, the patron saint of Wales and a pioneer of Christianity in Britain, was born near here early in the 6th century. He established the first monastery on this site. It remains the centre of all that is holy in Wales. The existing cathedral was begun in the late 12th century, by which time this remote Celtic outpost had become one of Europe's great pilgrimage sites. It's certainly worth pausing to explore the cathedral and the ruins of the Bishop's Palace.

The route crosses the River Alun and swings up, round the cathedral, through the towered gate into the city (actually no more than a large village). On the square, a one-way system takes you left and round the city. With a vibrant collection of cafés, art galleries, surf shops and restaurants, this is a great place to spend the night.

What to see

❶ Ocean Lab Entertaining marine-themed centre with café and internet access on the Parrog at Goodwick. *ocean-lab.co.uk*

❷ Royal Oak Inn Scene of the surrender in 1797 of a disenchanted ragtag French invading army and home to related memorabilia. The grave of local heroine Jemima Nicholas, who single-handedly captured 14 soldiers, is behind the pub. Tuesday night is folk night.

```
——— on-road
••••• traffic-free
```

St Davids Head

Whitesands Bay

Ramsey Island

Ramsey Sound

St Davids ❸

River Alun

Porthgain

Abereiddy Bay

Lla

Croes-goch

❹

A487

❸ St Davids Cathedral and Bishop's Palace An impressive manifestation of the medieval church's wealth and power, it was said by Pope Calixtus in 1124 that two pilgrimages to St Davids were the spiritual equivalent of one to Rome and three equal to one trip to Jerusalem. If you have the time, the guided tour is highly recommended. *stdavidscathedral.org.uk*

ℹ Tourist information centres can be found in Ocean Lab on the waterfront promenade at Goodwick and in the St Davids Visitor Centre just off the High Street in St Davids.

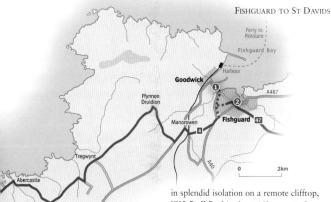

Where to stay

Down by Goodwick Harbour, before you climb the hill to Fishguard's town centre, you can bed down at the **Celtic Diving Base**, which is happy to accommodate cyclists as well as divers in its modern lodge house (*celticdiving.co.uk*). In Fishguard proper, **Hamilton Guest House and Backpackers Lodge** is a relaxed place close to the town centre and **Manor Town House**, while a little bit more expensive, has great views from the back bedrooms and a lovely terrace overlooking the harbour (*manortownhouse.com*). For campers, the route passes the front gate of well-run **Tregroes Touring and Camping Site** about 3km out of Fishguard. There are also a couple of hostels in the area which come highly recommended. Perched

in splendid isolation on a remote clifftop, **YHA Pwll Deri** is about 10km west of Fishguard (off-route) (*yha.org.uk*), while the charming and environmentally-friendly **Old School Hostel** (formerly YHA) in the village of Trefin is a lot easier to reach and well sited if you want to take it slow on this section (*theoldschoolhostel.co.uk*).

St Davids has a good mix of places to stay and caters well for walkers, cyclists and surfers. Recommended stops include the spacious **The Waterings** on the edge of town (*waterings.co.uk*) and the laid-back **TYF Eco Hotel** sited in a former windmill (*tyf.com*). Campers can enjoy the friendly cheese-producing **Caerfai Farm** (*cawscaerfai.co.uk*) or the well-appointed **Pencarnan Farm** (*stdavids.co.uk*), neither far from town. If you want to escape the summer crowds, **St Davids Youth Hostel** is based in an old farmhouse northwest of St Davids at Whitesands (*yha.org.uk*).

Spares and repairs

There are no bike shops on this section: make sure you are carrying all the spares you might need.

15

St Davids to Broad Haven

Distance 24km/15 miles (none traffic-free)
Terrain After an easy start, it turns hilly; all
on minor roads apart from 3km on a busy
A-road (there is a longer alternative route
to avoid this). No family-friendly sections
Time 2-3 hours Ascent 330m

**After the quiet, flat lanes between
St Davids and Newgale, the second
half of the ride comes as a shock:
you follow a lane that lurches up and
down the cliffs facing St Brides Bay.
Compensation comes in the form of
glorious views and some of the
wildest, most beautiful beaches in
western Britain.**

From the square, head east out of
St Davids on the High Street (A487).

As you leave town, by the school, fork left
on to a lane, 'Ffos y Mynach'. There are
great views south across St Brides Bay and
east towards the Preseli Hills. After 2km,
the lane skirts an old World War II airfield
where you might hear the ecstatic, bubbling
trill of skylarks. The decommissioned
airfield is now an organic hay meadow

and an important breeding ground for skylarks again.

The route wiggles through Whitchurch and drops down a steep hill to Middle Mill, where you can visit a traditional rug-making mill. Turn right here for a 3km round-trip diversion along the river, down to the delightful harbour at Solva, one of the best natural shelters on the Pembrokeshire coast: it's a hub of yachting activity with a variety of pubs, restaurants and craft shops.

After a short climb, Route 4 crosses more billiard table-flat farmland to reach a T-junction by a mobile holiday-home site and Brawdy Airfield. Turn right, and right again to reach the A487, where you turn left to Penycwm and the fast, steep descent to the beach at Newgale. An alternative longer and hillier route via quiet lanes starts at Penycwm – turn left where the main road bends right – rejoining the primary route on the coast 1km north of Nolton Haven.

After the tranquillity of the lanes, the noise of the A487 and the plummeting descent to Newgale Sands are a sensory power surge. But the vast expanse of white-capped surf and sand is a great sight and soon enough Route 4 leaves the roaring traffic behind again: turn right at the end of the beach by a public car park, towards Nolton Haven. Here you cross an unmarked border, the Landsker Line, which divides the

Welsh-speaking, often wild and sometimes remote north half of Pembrokeshire from the prettified, wealthier south, which is known as 'Little England beyond Wales'. This abrupt division, which runs roughly from Newgale to Carmarthen, dates from the early medieval period when the Normans invaded and occupied southern Pembrokeshire because of its strategic importance, repopulating the area with Anglo-Saxons and Flemish. Today, the division is far from obvious, though there are subtle changes in the landscape, the architecture and the accents.

A delightful lane hugs the coast, rising and falling with chest-tightening regularity all the way to Broad Haven. From the high cliffs, there are grand views across the whole of St Brides Bay, from Ramsey Island round to Skomer Island. The sheltered coves and sweeping beaches are almost irresistible – if the sun is shining, this is a place to linger.

A fast descent leads down to Nolton Haven, an idyllic cove with a beach and a pub. Climbing steeply out of the village, don't miss the right fork to Druidston Haven. To visit the beach at Druidston Haven, you have to park your bike in a hedgerow and walk. At low tide, it's worth the effort – a mile of golden sand with rockpools and caves, banked by steep cliffs. The water quality is very good, though swimmers should beware of strong currents. The Druidstone Hotel above the beach is a good spot to refresh, particularly if you arrive here in the evening and the sun is setting on the sea.

There is one more climb. At the T-junction turn right and race down the hill to the seafront and beach in Broad Haven. Route 4 turns left abruptly at the bottom of the hill: continue straight on if you're stopping. Little Haven, a cosy fishing village, is 1km further on.

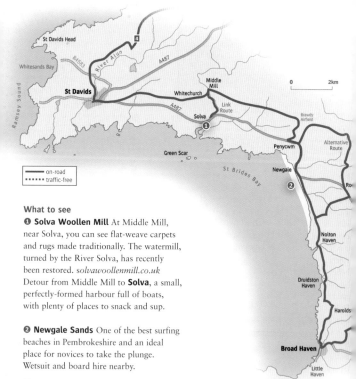

What to see

❶ Solva Woollen Mill At Middle Mill, near Solva, you can see flat-weave carpets and rugs made traditionally. The watermill, turned by the River Solva, has recently been restored. *solvawoollenmill.co.uk* Detour from Middle Mill to **Solva**, a small, perfectly-formed harbour full of boats, with plenty of places to snack and sup.

❷ Newgale Sands One of the best surfing beaches in Pembrokeshire and an ideal place for novices to take the plunge. Wetsuit and board hire nearby.

Where to stay

Broad Haven and the surrounding area is popular with holidaying families and can get very busy in summer, so make sure you book in advance wherever you plan to stay. If you are on a budget and just want a bunk then head for **Broad Haven Youth Hostel**, a large modern bungalow complex with more than 70 beds and a good café very close to the sands of St Brides Bay (*yha.org.uk*). For a welcoming B&B, the **Anchor Guest House** is hard to beat, being right on the route – and the beach (*anchorguesthouse.co.uk*). If you would rather get under canvas then the popular **Nolton Cross Caravan Park** is about 4km inland from Nolton Haven (*noltoncross-holidays.co.uk*) and the equally functional **South Cockett Campsite** is not far from Broad Haven on the road to Haverfordwest (*southcockett.co.uk*).

If you want to savour this stretch of the route and you like stunning sea views and good home-made food then pull in at the colourful **Druidstone Hotel** located on the grassy cliffs above the glorious beach of Druidston Haven, 4km north of Broad Haven (*druidstone.co.uk*). Alternatively, if you plan to take your time reaching Broad Haven then you could break your journey earlier in the village of Solva where you will find several good B&Bs as well as pubs, cafés and restaurants (*solva.net*). Further on, **Newgale Camping Site** is also an excellent place to enjoy the glorious Pembrokeshire coastline (*newgalecampingsite.co.uk*).

Spares and repairs

No bike shops: make sure you are carrying all the spares you might need.

19

Broad Haven to Tenby

Distance **46km/29 miles (14km traffic-free)** Terrain **The only major climb is first thing, out of Broad Haven. After that, the route rolls gently along minor roads with one excellent 12km section of cyclepath, following a railway line between Haverfordwest and Neyland – ideal for a family day out** Time **4 hours** Ascent **340m**

Leaving behind the dramatic seascapes of the Pembrokeshire coast, you head inland to Haverfordwest, the functional county town. Part of Brunel's great London to Neyland railway line spits you out on Milford Haven. Having skirted the magnificent castle at Pembroke, an ancient road follows the high ground to Tenby.

Route 4 climbs away from the sea at the northern end of the promenade in Broad Haven on the B4341. Halfway up the hill, look for the left turn on to Long Lane. At the top of a 1km straight, turn right and return to the B4341. A new cyclepath beside the main road heads through the village, Portfield Gate.

At the next row of houses, turn right down a lane and go straight on at the crossroads. You are skirting the southwest corner of Haverfordwest. At the next left hand bend opposite a sports field, turn right – this is easy to miss – down a 'No through road'. You arrive at the bottom of the valley by a bridge. Cross over for Neyland and Tenby. Or go straight on for 2.5km, with the river on your right initially, then on a

cyclepath along the A4076, to reach the centre of Haverfordwest.

The cyclepath veers southwest and climbs steadily alongside the current railway line, through a fine stand of beech, to reach Johnston. Continue straight on to join the disused railway line. A century and a half ago, this was the final section of Brunel's remarkable engineering project, the Great Western Railway, from Paddington to the terminus at Neyland. The tarmac trail winds gently downhill and through Westfield Pill Nature Reserve on a limestone dust surface (to protect the rare plants). It's a lovely ride.

Just before you pass under the Cleddau Bridge, Route 4 takes a sharp right up the steep bank to the main road. If you continue 200m under the bridge, you come to the excellent café at Neyland Marina on Brunel Quay.

At the top of the steep bank, cross over the A477, turn left and continue on a cycle lane over two bridges. There are fine views over Milford Haven, one of the finest inlets of deep water in the British Isles: today, its primary function is as an oil port, but it's also been home to whaling stations and great naval shipyards, as well as the launching and landing place of several invasions. Beware – it can be extremely windy on the bridge.

On the south side of the bridge, Route 4 winds round Pembroke Dock, where five royal yachts were built in the 19th century. The signs are difficult to spot, so keep the

▲ Sunset at Broad Haven

21

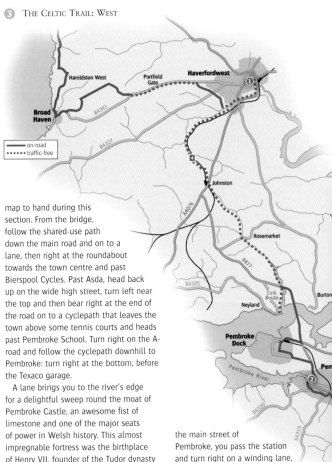

map to hand during this
section. From the bridge,
follow the shared-use path
down the main road and on to a
lane, then right at the roundabout
towards the town centre and past
Bierspool Cycles. Past Asda, head back
up on the wide high street, turn left near
the top and then bear right at the end of
the road on to a cyclepath that leaves the
town above some tennis courts and heads
past Pembroke School. Turn right on the A-
road and follow the cyclepath downhill to
Pembroke: turn right at the bottom, before
the Texaco garage.

A lane brings you to the river's edge
for a delightful sweep round the moat of
Pembroke Castle, an awesome fist of
limestone and one of the major seats
of power in Welsh history. This almost
impregnable fortress was the birthplace
of Henry VII, founder of the Tudor dynasty
and the first Welshman to sit on the
English throne.

Heading east, through a park beside the
remains of the town walls and then up to

the main street of
Pembroke, you pass the station
and turn right on a winding lane,
speeding alongside the railway line to
Lamphey. Turn left, cross the railway line
again and take the first right towards the
ruins of Lamphey Palace, a retreat for the

22

What to see

❶ Haverfordwest Castle and the Museum both bring to light some of Pembrokeshire's rich history. The ruined priory is beside the River Cleddau, formerly navigable from the sea and key to the town's prosperity in the Middle Ages. Nearby is the Bristol Trader, a medieval pub full of character. *haverfordwest-town-museum.org.uk*

❷ Pembroke Castle is very well preserved, despite being bombarded by Cromwell during the English Civil War. It's also fascinating. Climb the late 12th-century keep for great views of Milford Haven, or have a picnic on the lawn. *pembroke-castle.co.uk*

❸ Tenby The pastel-painted town of Tenby is delightful, even when it's teeming with tourists. Wander among the Georgian facades, cobbled alleys and cockeyed gables inside the 15th-century town walls, down to the harbour, back up to the Tudor Merchant's House and down again to one of the beaches. Augustus John, the formative early 20th-century artist, was born here. The Plantagenet House restaurant is a unique place to dine. *virtualtenby.co.uk*

❹ Caldey Island There are daily boat trips to Caldey Island from Tenby – it's a tranquil place, as you might expect the home of monks for 1500 years to be. *caldey-island.co.uk*

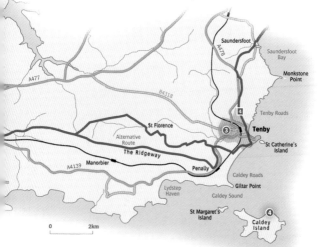

bishops of St Davids dating from the 13th century and abandoned to the ivy during the Reformation.

After a long, gradual climb, Route 4 emerges on the Ridgeway, a lane following the course of a Neolithic track along the high ground to Penally. There are expansive views across the rich, green farmland of southern Pembrokeshire and the mouth of the Bristol Channel to Devon and Cornwall. Just over 3km from Lamphey, Route 4 turns left. You can – and it's certainly worth it if the wind is behind you – stay on the Ridgeway all the way to Penally, where the road descends dramatically and sweeps round north, through the town to rejoin Route 4 before crossing the A4139.

If you wish to stay on Route 4, leave the Ridgeway and take the first right and then,

after 1.5km, another right – both easy to miss when you're rattling downhill – into St Florence. Encouraged by the Norman hegemony in the 12th century, many Flemings immigrated to this area and built their distinctive 'Flemish chimneys', some of which remain. There are pubs and a shop in this pretty village.

Much of the run down to cross the A4139 is a lovely twisting descent on narrow lanes. Once over the main road, head through Kiln Park Campsite to the beach, cross the railway line and follow the track beside Tenby's famous links golf course. A short, steep climb brings you up from South Beach – tough to resist if it's sunny – to the Esplanade. There are fine views of Caldey Island. Turn left down the one-way circuit to go into town.

Tenby harbour ▶

◀ Pembroke Castle

Where to stay

If the busy resort of Tenby is your intended stop then remember to book ahead and, if you can, avoid weekends. There are dozens of B&Bs and small hotels to choose from as well as quite a few campsites near the town. Of the guesthouses, friendly **Osnock** on Southcliff, **Croyland** on Harding Street, near the railway station (*thecroyland.co.uk*) and the functional **Weybourne Guest House** (*weybourneguesthouse.co.uk*) are among the cycle-friendly. **Kiln Park Campsite** is well situated right on the route as you enter Tenby if you would rather camp.

If you are taking your time on this section then other good B&B options on route include the **College Guest House**, a Georgian townhouse in Haverfordwest (*collegeguesthouse.com*) and the splendidly welcoming and civilised **Penfro Guest House** in Pembroke (*penfro.co.uk*).

Spares and repairs

Mikes Bikes in Haverfordwest, **Enterprise Bikes** in Honeyborough, Neyland, **Bierspool Cycles** in Pembroke Dock and **Tenby Cycles** on The Norton in Tenby will all endeavour to keep you on the road.

Tourist information centres can be found at Old Bridge in Haverfordwest and in Upper Park Road, Tenby.

Tenby to Laugharne

Distance **26km/16 miles (2km traffic-free)**
Terrain **Apart from two short sections
of traffic-free, shared-use path that hug
the bay between Saundersfoot and Amroth
– ideal for a short family ride – the section
is predominantly on minor roads. Three
significant climbs: the first straight out of
Tenby and two between Amroth and
Laugharne** Time **3 hours 30** Ascent **380m**

**Two of South Wales' prettiest seaside
towns connected by three teeth-gritting
climbs. The long descent into Laugharne
is wonderful.**

From South Beach Esplanade, follow signs
through the old town walls, left along the
High Street and Norton Road, above the
harbour and North Beach. When the road
dips and swings left, look for a right turn up
Slippery Back: the lane rises steeply to the
cemetery and joins a track. Bear right on
the A478: the route weaves alongside it,
over a roundabout (turn right) and then
right, downhill to Saundersfoot with lovely
views of the bay ahead.

On the seafront in Saundersfoot, turn
left: there are various places to rest and
refresh in this bustling family holiday resort.
At the end of the road, you have to
dismount to pass through the tunnels on
the Pembrokeshire Coast Path National Trail
– the renowned 299km footpath, which you
share as far as Amroth. The shared-use path
follows the route of an old tramway to

◄ The beach at Amroth

Wiseman's Bridge, along which coal (high-quality anthracite) was transported to Saundersfoot for export in the 19th century.

Winston Churchill took tea at the Inn at Wiseman's Bridge in 1943 with General Eisenhower and General Montgomery, having watched 100,000 men storm the beaches between Pendine and Saundersfoot: it was a dress rehearsal for the D-Day Landings.

Route 4 ascends steeply on the road out of Wiseman's Bridge. Look out for the right turn up Cliff Road – it's easy to miss when you're grinding away on the pedals with your head hung low – which leads on to a lovely section along the clifftops, high above the sea, with views across the great sweep of Carmarthen Bay to Pembrey and the Gower Peninsula.

There's a fast descent to Amroth. Ride along the seafront to Amroth Castle (pub) and the start of the first long climb. Here you leave behind the busy, eclectic tourist centres of Pembrokeshire and enter an altogether different and delightful place – rural Carmarthenshire. The lanes empty of vehicles; farmyard smells and birdsong magically return.

At Marros Church, the road descends steeply into a wooded valley and, just beyond the Green Bridge Inn, turn left and start to climb again. Almost 1km beyond the crossroads with the B4314, an alternative signed route bears left at the fork: this is a shortcut, missing out Laugharne to head straight for St Clears. Carry straight on for a long, glorious descent, bearing right and right again, all the way to the picturesque town of Laugharne, beside the Taf Estuary. The lane brings you out beside the castle.

For several years, Laugharne was home to Dylan Thomas, the sensual, melancholy, characteristically Welsh genius. Though he died in New York, he's buried here in the churchyard of St Martin's, and the fictional village in *Under Milk Wood*, Llareggub, will forever be associated with Laugharne. The Boathouse, "sea shaken on a breakneck of rocks," beside the "Heron-priested" River Taf, where Thomas lived with his family, is now a heritage centre and a lot better organised than the poet himself ever was. If you're interested in Thomas, or more widely in poetry as part of the Welsh condition, it's a must-see. The town is full of places to refresh any parts the poets can't reach: Brown's, where Thomas quaffed pints daily, is on the main street.

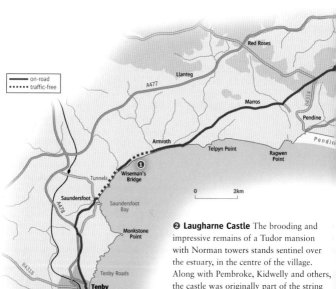

on-road
traffic-free

Red Roses

Llanteg

A477

Marros

Pendine

B4314

Armroth

Telpyn Point

Ragwen Point

Pendi

Tunnels

Wiseman's Bridge ❶

0   2km

Saundersfoot

Saundersfoot Bay

Monkstone Point

B4318

Tenby Roads

Tenby

St Catherine's Island

4

Alternative Route

ℹ️ Tourist information is available from the office at the harbour in Saundersfoot, and from Corran Books in Laugharne.

What to see

❶ Saundersfoot, Coppet Hall, Glen, Wiseman's Bridge, Amroth The chain of beaches along the first half of this section are broad, sheltered, sandy and most of them are connected at low tide.

❷ Laugharne Castle The brooding and impressive remains of a Tudor mansion with Norman towers stands sentinel over the estuary, in the centre of the village. Along with Pembroke, Kidwelly and others, the castle was originally part of the string of coastal strongholds by which the Normans held Southwest Wales. If the sun is shining, the Victorian garden inside the castle grounds is a lovely spot for a picnic.

❸ The Boathouse where Dylan Thomas lived and wrote *Under Milk Wood* is down a narrow lane, on Cliff Road in Laugharne. It's an enchanting museum overlooking the ever-shifting estuary. Thomas' writing shed, built on stilts, is as the poet left it. Thomas and his widow Caitlin are buried in a grave marked by a modest white wooden cross in the churchyard of St Martin's Church on the northern edge of town. *dylanthomasboathouse.com*

Laugharne Castle ▶

Laugharne Sands

Where to stay

There is no shortage of guesthouses and caravan parks along the coast as you pass through Saundersfoot, Wiseman's Bridge and Amroth. Turning inland and away from the tourist hubs, there is less choice so booking ahead is advisable. In Laugharne, Dylan Thomas' "timeless, mild, beguiling island of a town", the suitably relaxed **Laugharne Coach House**, with its balcony overlooking the bay, is an excellent place to rest up. The **New Three Mariners** also has pretty much everything you could want in a B&B (*newthreemariners.co.uk*). For campers, there are a few caravan parks not far from Laugharne where you can pitch up: the two closest are **Broadway Caravan Park** off the A4066 just south of town and **Ants Hill Caravan Park** on the way to St Clears (*antshill.co.uk*).

Spares and repairs

There are no bike shops on this section.

Laugharne to Carmarthen

Distance 30km/18.5 miles (2km traffic-free) Terrain Rolling countryside, mainly on quiet lanes; one section of cyclepath beside the busy A40 and one notable climb between St Clears and Carmarthen Time 3 hours Ascent 330m

Route 4 diverts inland, looping north round the broad twin estuaries of the Taf and the Towy. The small triangle of land bordered by these rivers and the A40 is delightfully quiet and rural, harking back to post-war Britain.

From Laugharne Castle, follow the main street north out of town and continue on the A4066 for 1.5km to Cross Inn: it's not a busy A-road, but still, take care. Bear left at the obvious fork in Cross Inn onto a lane.

After 2km, bear right and you come to a small crossroads. The alternative shortcut, avoiding Laugharne, rejoins Route 4 here. Turn right towards the brow of the hill: there is a steep descent ahead.

This lane returns to the A4066, crossing the River Taf and entering the predominantly Welsh-speaking town of St Clears. Leave the Celtic Trail and continue over the A40 if you want to visit the shops or the noted chippy – there's nothing else until Carmarthen – and take your lunch down to the riverbank. Route 4 heads east along the south side of the A40 – a dual carriageway and often roaringly

busy – along a cyclepath for about 2km. It's a section to put your head down.

Take heart, though: when you do leave the main road, turning right down a lane to head south, you might not see another car for several kilometres. This triangle of land bordered by the Taf, the Towy and the A40 seems to have been overlooked by the second half of the 20th century. The tapestry of modest-sized fields and hedgerows bursting with birds is dotted with shabby farmsteads and chapels, and sliced with innumerable streams trickling south. It's as if time stood still here in about 1945.

You cross the River Cywyn at Pont-ddu, turn left and climb steeply: it's quite a haul to Llangynog. Follow signs through the village and turn right at College Farm to speed down and clamber out of a wooded valley. Then as the lanes begin to gather together, so you gain momentum and suddenly you're flying downhill into an industrial estate on the edge of Carmarthen.

Turn left on the B4312, cross the A40 on the flyover and turn right at traffic lights up Monument Hill. At the utilitarian Inland Revenue building on Picton Terrace, turn right – easy to miss – and enter Carmarthen Park. Go round the velodrome (reputedly the oldest in Wales), through another industrial estate, cross the main road and head along the river to reach the new footbridge over the Towy. The centre of town is beyond the main road; the railway station is across the footbridge.

The Romans built their most westerly camp beside the Towy Estuary here and Carmarthen has been the county town since Norman times. Though it's difficult to imagine today, Carmarthen was the biggest town in Wales for a brief period in the 18th century, on account of the wool trade, and some of the elegant Georgian buildings are thought to have been designed by John Nash. Throw in the mythical birthplace of the Celtic magician, Merlin (the Welsh for Carmarthen – 'Caerfyrddin' – means 'Merlin's Fort), and the reputation in Tudor times as the most inebriated town in Wales, and Carmarthen becomes a colourful place. If you've followed Route 4 thus far, this might also be the first place you hear the native language spoken. Between the ruined castle, the Roman Amphitheatre and the craft galleries, there's plenty to keep you entertained for an afternoon.

Two major Celtic Trail loops, using Routes 4 and 47, start and finish in Carmarthen. The circuit of West Wales that makes best use of the prevailing winds (and gets the hard bit out of the way first) heads north-west from Carmarthen on Route 47 over the Preseli Hills to Fishguard, and then back to Carmarthen on Route 4 via St Davids, Tenby and Laugharne (230km). The second loop heads east on Route 47 via the National Botanic Garden of Wales to Llanelli and along Route 4 via Kidwelly to Carmarthen (140km). Carmarthen has a good train service to Swansea, Cardiff and beyond.

◄ The Boathouse at Laugharne

What to see

❶ Carmarthen Castle

The strategic importance of Carmarthen was such that the Normans built a castle here at the end of the 11th century. The first major rebuild, in stone, was completed in 1233. Of course, it was duly and intermittently sacked by the Welsh (Llewelyn the Great in 1215 and Owain Glyndwr in 1405) and refortified on several occasions before being badly damaged during the English Civil War. The gatehouse, keep, two towers and a section of curtain wall are all that remain, but it's worth a visit, if only for the grand views over the Towy.

❷ Oriel Myrddin Gallery exhibits and sells the finest contemporary Welsh crafts. *orielmyrddingallery.co.uk*

❸ Roman Amphitheatre

The Romans called their strategic camp on the Towy Estuary 'Moridunum': all that remains of this extreme western outpost of the Empire is the site of an amphitheatre, 1km north of the town centre.

🛈 Carmarthen's **tourist information centre** is on Lammas Street.

Boar's Head Hotel (*boarsheadhotel.com*) and the equally historic **Drovers Arms Hotel** (*droversarmshotel.com*), both on Lammas Street in the centre of Carmarthen, welcome cyclists. There are also several guesthouses to choose from: among them **Y Dderwen Fach** is cosy, good value and close to the amphitheatre.

Spares and repairs

Hobbs Bikes, across the Towy and tucked in beside Currys, is just metres from Route 47. Full repairs and spares available. Also in Carmarthen, there's a **Halfords** Superstore at Parc Pensarn.

Where to stay

There are plenty of places to eat, drink and sleep in and around the bustling county town of Carmarthen. The 17th-century

Fishguard to Crymych

Distance 34km/21.5 miles (none traffic-free) Terrain All on quiet B-roads or sleepy lanes, through relentlessly hilly countryside. No family-friendly sections Time 4 hours Ascent 580m

A strenuous section – there's scarcely a flat kilometre – through wild and magnificent Pembrokeshire countryside, into the heart of the Preseli Hills. Outside conservative pub hours, there's almost nowhere to eat and drink once you've left Fishguard: carry all the sustenance you need.

As with Route 4, Route 47 starts beside the Irish Sea at Ocean Lab (tourist information centre and café), the modern building on Goodwick Harbour. From the railway station and the Fishguard-Rosslare

ferry terminal, follow the road inland with the cliffs on your right, past the ferry office to the roundabout: Ocean Lab is in front of you. Pick up the cyclepath here, heading along the front, away from the terminals and uphill beside the A40.

The cyclepath leaves the main road, crosses a minor road and climbs again through a clump of pine trees to a junction where Routes 47 and 4 split for the first time: turn left for Route 47 (and Route 82 to Cardigan). A cyclepath brings you back into Fishguard town: turn right on the main street. It's worth pausing to look around Fishguard, famed as the site of the last invasion of Britain in 1797: a ragged French army was forced to surrender by the local militia and their brawny womenfolk. The old harbour is 500m below the main street, at

◀ On the way to Crymych

the mouth of the River Gwaun. The glitzy 1971 version of *Under Milk Wood* starring Richard Burton and Elizabeth Taylor was filmed around this picturesque port.

Turn left at the roundabout in front of the town hall and, after 50m, right into Hamilton Street. Take the first left, on the B4313 and climb gently out of town. Quickly, the nature of the countryside reveals itself. This is a wild Celtic realm with signature features – unkempt, whitewashed farmsteads sunk into the hillsides, sod hedges sprouting vivid yellow, coconut-scented gorse, antique stone walls, stunted wind-bent trees and fuschia bushes. At the top of the climb, there are wonderful views northeast to Dinas Head and Fishguard Bay and southeast to the weathered tors of the Preseli Hills.

The B4313 swoops down into the steep-sided, thickly-wooded Gwaun Valley – apparently Europe's oldest glacial vale – and past the pub in Llanychaer. The climb out of the valley is the longest of the day: 3km after Llanychaer, Route 47 turns right on to a lane, towards Puncheston. It's uphill for a further 2km. (Route 82 – the 158km route through Cardigan and the Teifi Valley to Aberystwyth – continues straight on here, following the Gwaun Valley.)

The views from the flanks of Mynydd Cilciffeth (334m), at the top of the climb, are terrific: the land seems to slope gently all the way down to

St Davids Head, and you can see half of Pembrokeshire on a clear day. On a lane with grass growing out of the tarmac, you whistle down to Puncheston. Turn right into the village and left just before the Drovers Arms, towards Tufton.

Go straight on at the crossroads in Tufton, by the Tufton Arms, and down the hill. A sharp left brings you back up to meet another quiet lane which rejoins the B4313 after 3km. Turn left and, after 500m, right towards Crymych on a lane that skirts round the heights of the Preseli Hills: Foel Cwmcerwyn, the highest point at 536m, is just to the north of the route here and the Preseli ridge runs east of it. With excellent visibility, you can see from the Gower Peninsula to the Llyn Peninsula – practically the length of Wales –

35

from the top of Foel Cwmcerwyn.

There are standing stones, tumuli, cairns, cromlechs and burial chambers galore, scattered across this ancient landscape. With an OS map to hand, it is well worth exploring some of these prehistoric sites on foot. Just before the village of Mynachlog-ddu, a path leads up to Carn Menyn: it is believed the 'bluestones' used to construct the inner circle of Stonehenge came from this crag-edged promontory of rock. Quite how prehistoric man got them from here to Salisbury Plain remains a matter of conjecture.

From Mynachlog-ddu, Route 47 continues northeast, past Llethr plantation and downhill to Crymych (Welsh for 'crooked stream'). Turn left on the A478 into the centre of town to reach the Crymych Arms Inn. This tiny town is the biggest conurbation between Fishguard and Carmarthen and it retains a strong sense of identity based on Welsh language and culture. The places to stay are outside the town, but stock up in the shops for the onward journey to Carmarthen.

i Fishguard's **tourist information centre** can be found in Ocean Lab on the waterfront promenade at Goodwick.

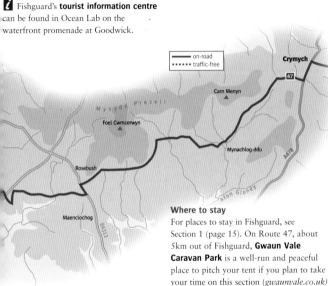

on-road
traffic-free

What to see

1 Ocean Lab Entertaining marine-themed centre with café and internet access on the Parrog at Goodwick. ocean-lab.co.uk

2 Royal Oak Inn Scene of the surrender in 1797 of a disenchanted ragtag French invading army and home to related memorabilia. The grave of local heroine Jemima Nicholas, who single-handedly captured 14 soldiers, is behind the pub. Tuesday night is folk night.

Where to stay

For places to stay in Fishguard, see Section 1 (page 15). On Route 47, about 5km out of Fishguard, **Gwaun Vale Caravan Park** is a well-run and peaceful place to pitch your tent if you plan to take your time on this section (*gwaunvale.co.uk*). Further on, bed and breakfast can be had at **Penygraig Farmhouse** at Puncheston, **Twmpath Guest House** at Maenclochog (*twmpath.co.uk*) and **Dolau Isaf Farm** at Mynachlog-ddu (*farmhouse accommodation.net*). There are no guesthouses in Crymych, but you could push on down the road for B&B at the award-winning **Butchers Arms** in Tegryn (*butchers-arms.net*).

Spares and repairs

There are no bike shops on this section.

Crymych to Carmarthen

Distance **39km/24 miles** (none traffic-free)
Terrain **Tough undulating section, mostly
on quiet lanes. No family-friendly sections**
Time **4 hours** Ascent **520m**

**Another tough section, up and down the
steep-sided 'cwms' or valleys of this
delightfully rural part of West Wales.
You pass only a couple of pubs and
shops: stock up in Crymych before
setting off.**

From the Crymych Arms Inn, follow the
A487 north out of town and take the first
right after 100m onto a lane signed
'Tegryn.' After 3km, look out for another
right turn as you're speeding downhill.
Turn right again at the next T-junction.
Pass the Butchers Arms in Tegryn and
drop down the hill, past the primary
school, taking the first left as the road rises.

Tegryn claims to be the highest village in
Pembrokeshire and it's said you can see
Snowdon on a perfectly clear day. Certainly
the views north across the Cych and Teifi
Valleys from the ridge leading over Rhos-y-
Llyn, 1km beyond the village, are
tremendous, especially when the wind is
blowing and clouds are scudding overhead.
Go straight on at the next crossroads and
swiftly downhill: bear left to cross a stream
– the border between Pembrokeshire and
Carmarthenshire – and take the right fork
up a sharp hill that'll have you crashing
through the gears.

Just as you've got your breath back at the
top, you're off again, whooshing down to
the hamlet of Dinas. An abandoned
medieval mill here hints at the power

◄ On the road to Trelech

contained in the lattice of streams that teem out of these hills, filling the River Teifi to the north and the Cleddau and Taf to the south. And it's these streams, or at least the tear-inducing descents and the heart-stopping ascents in and out of the valleys they've created, that are the geographical refrain for this section of the Celtic Trail.

At the top of the climb out of Dinas, turn left at the T-junction and drop down into the pretty village of Trelech: with a pub and a shop, this is the busiest community until Carmarthen. Turn right beside the chapel onto the B4299 and, after 200m of climbing, turn left. The lane wiggles away, dropping once to cross the Dewi Fawr River, before returning to this picturesque valley as it dashes through the village of Pen-y-bont.

On these quiet lanes and among the remote farmsteads with their unconverted barns, muddy yards and rusting old Ferguson tractors, there's a sense of time standing still here.

Following a long descent and an even longer climb – at 2.5km, this one gets a special mention – through a wooded valley with the village of Talog (shop) at the bottom, you emerge onto a high north-facing ridge. There are grand views all the way back to the Preseli Hills. Turn left at the next T-junction and right after 400m onto a lane that starts to run gently downhill: 100m after the hamlet of Knightsford Farm, turn left, signposted

'Bronwydd'. You are at the end of this range of hills and the views open out east towards the glacier-sculpted heights of the Carmarthen Fans.

A very fast 3km descent brings you to Bronwydd Arms. Turn right on the A484 and almost immediately left, over the River Gwili to climb steeply up the valley: fork right half way up. This lane descends, following the river, to meet the A485 on the outskirts of Carmarthen. Go straight over two roundabouts and sharp left at the third, then right onto a cyclepath before the flyover.

Follow the dual carriageway past the ruins of Carmarthen Priory on your right, as far as the Esplanade, a row of handsome Georgian houses overlooking an elegant loop of the River Towy. Cross the lane and follow another cyclepath beneath County Hall, through the back of an industrial estate and up to a main road. The town centre is straight ahead. Turn left, over the river and immediately right, past the railway station to reach the new footbridge over the Towy, where Routes 4 and 47 rejoin and this section ends.

If you are riding the loop of West Wales from Carmarthen to Fishguard on Route 47 and back, via St Davids, Tenby and Laugharne on Route 4, your journey starts here and you have to follow this section (and Section 6) backwards. Carmarthen has a good train service to Swansea, Cardiff and beyond.

What to see

❶ Caws Cenarth Farm

Some 7km north of Route 47 from Tegryn, you can see Welsh farmhouse Caerphilly cheese made traditionally by hand. *cawscenarth.co.uk*

❷ Gwili Steam Railway

The volunteer-run steam train operates from Bronwydd Arms Station, through the wooded valley to Danycoed Halt. The round-trip takes about an hour, or longer if you stop for a picnic. *gwili-railway.co.uk*

🛈 Carmarthen's **tourist information centre** is on Lammas Street.

Spares and repairs

Hobbs Bikes, across the Towy and tucked in beside Currys, is just metres from Route 47. Full repairs and spares available. Also in Carmarthen, there's a **Halfords** Superstore at Parc Pensarn.

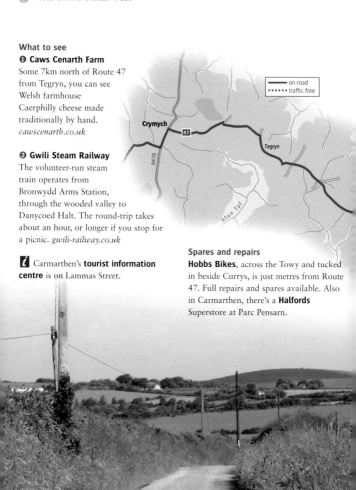

❸ Carmarthen Castle

The strategic importance of Carmarthen was such that the Normans built a castle here at the end of the 11th century. The first major rebuild, in stone, was completed in 1233. Of course, it was duly and intermittently sacked by the Welsh (Llewelyn the Great in 1215 and Owain Glyndwr in 1405) and refortified on several occasions before being badly damaged during the English Civil War. The gatehouse, keep, two towers and a section of curtain wall are all that remain, but it's worth a visit, if only for the grand views over the Towy.

❹ Oriel Myrddin Gallery exhibits and sells the finest contemporary Welsh crafts.
orielmyrddingallery.co.uk

❺ Roman Amphitheatre

The Romans called their strategic camp on the Towy Estuary 'Moridunum': all that remains of this extreme western outpost of the Empire is the site of an amphitheatre, 1km north of the town centre.

Where to stay

Not far from Crymych, the excellent **Butchers Arms** in Tegryn does B&B (*butchers-arms.net*), otherwise there are no guesthouses until Carmarthen. For accommodation in Carmarthen see Section 5 (page 33).

◀ Quiet roads on Route 47

Carmarthen to Swansea via Kidwelly

Distance **69km/43 miles (35km traffic-free)** Terrain **A hilly start on minor roads as far as Kidwelly; after that, it's predominantly traffic-free, flat and ideal for children. From Kidwelly to Llanelli, Gowerton or even Swansea, returning by train, would make a superb family ride** Time **5 hours** Ascent **250m**

Once you've conquered the hills between Carmarthen and Kidwelly, you're on the easiest section of the entire Celtic Trail. Gravel trails through Pembrey Forest bring you to the Millennium Coastal Park – an outstanding regeneration project that hugs the Burry Estuary for over 20km. The last section, from Gowerton to Swansea Bay through the Clyne Valley is also traffic-free.

Following Route 4 out of Carmarthen is tricky: from the footbridge over the River Towy, pass the railway station, turn right on the main road and go straight on at the roundabout along Stephens Way. Pass under the A484, turn right under another main road and pick up the cyclepath along the A484 for 1km, south to Pibwrlwyd. (Try saying that in a hurry – if nothing else, the Celtic Trail is a good introduction to the ancient, unpronounceable poetry of Welsh place names.) At the roundabout, turn right onto a minor road towards Croesyceiliog, leaving the noisy traffic behind.

A 1km-long tough climb brings you back up to the A484, which you follow for 500m. It's not a busy A-road, but it's fast. Turn right towards Towy Castle Care Home and look out for the sharp left hand bend on the descent. The lane rises and falls before a long, fast plunge down a thickly-wooded dell to Ferryside. Of course, the ferry (across the Towy Estuary to Llansteffan) no longer runs and this small town has a slightly forgotten air. There is a pub by the railway station, and some say the fish and chips from The Ferry Cabin are the best in Wales.

The lane hugs the coast, climbing steeply

◀ Ferryside

onto the cliffs above the Gwendraeth Estuary, past a large holiday home park before gently descending to a nature reserve and Kidwelly. There's an Industrial Museum here – a good place to brush up for the journey ahead into the heartland of post-industrial Wales – but the main attraction is Kidwelly Castle. Once again founded by the Anglo-Normans to subdue the Welsh, it squats magnificently above a bend in the Gwendreath Fach River. The early 15th-century gatehouse is remarkably well preserved.

Turn right on Route 4 to cross the river on the medieval bridge: there are pubs and a good cyclists café on the main street. Head south, keeping to the signs, to meet the A484 again, and follow a cyclepath for 500m until a right turn leads under the railway and on to a great expanse of marshland, dykes and crumbling runways. The next 27km are almost entirely traffic-free.

RAF Pembrey was an important airbase during World War II. Much of it is now a conservation site and the 1000-hectare pine forest on the sand dunes is a botanist's delight. Listen for the songbirds at dawn and dusk, and look out for the rare butterflies and orchids. The trails, on gravel and grass, weave towards the coast at Pembrey Country Park. You can detour here to a lovely beach or continue east through the Millennium Coastal Park.

The Millennium Coastal Park is the result of one of the greatest coastal regeneration stories in Britain: 1500 acres of Victorian steel mills, tinplate works, hills of ash, slag heaps and other industrial jetsam have been transformed into a space where nature is reasserting its primacy. The park incorporates the National Wetland Centre for Wales, numerous visitor attractions, some fine sculptures and the wonderful, continuous cycle trail. With sunlight playing on the riddled, corrugated sands of the Burry Estuary and views across to the Gower Peninsula, it really is a joy.

There are good cafés at the sail-shaped Park Discovery Centre (500m from Llanelli train station) and at the Wildfowl and Wetlands Centre (just off the route but worth a detour). The traffic-free section finally, sadly, ends when you cross the railway line and the A484. Via a side street that runs parallel, you return to the A484 to cross the Loughor Bridge. Bear left at the roundabout over the bridge and take the

first right on to Pont Y Cob Road, which dips back under the railway and along a saltmarsh into Gowerton. For a highly recommended detour west, round the Gower Peninsula – one of Britain's most beautiful protuberances, where Dylan Thomas used to take his "Devils for an airing" – follow the B4295 at the end of Pont Y Cob Road towards Crofty, along the North Gower Trail. To continue on Route 4, turn left and follow the B4295 to Gowerton railway station, then turn right and immediately left on to an old railway line. There is a short diversion from the disused railway through a housing estate – pay attention to the signs – before you start

climbing steadily towards Dunvant.

At the Railway Inn, the tarmac path starts to gently descend through the Clyne Valley. At the bottom of this thick broadleaf wood, you abruptly arrive at Black Pill and the busy A4067 on Swansea Bay: turn right for the Junction Box Café (50m) and the Victorian seaside resort of Mumbles, once famous for its oyster beds. Turn left along the seafront to Swansea, following the route of the old Mumbles passenger train.

The "ugly, lovely" city, as Dylan Thomas wrote of Swansea, has in recent decades worked hard to slough off its industrial legacy: not easy, since this was the world's

leading copper-producing region for over a century. Being flattened during the Blitz in 1941 didn't help Wales' second city, but the Maritime Quarter has been the subject of a major rebuild and is becoming fashionable again.

Route 4 leaves the seafront just before reaching the mouth of the River Tawe: turn left, cross Trawler Road and a footbridge over the marina – it's hard to spot the signs – to reach the Sail Bridge over the Tawe and the end of this section. Route 43, which will eventually connect Swansea with Brecon and Builth Wells in mid-Wales, meets Route 4 here. The museums, the railway station and the shops are all nearby.

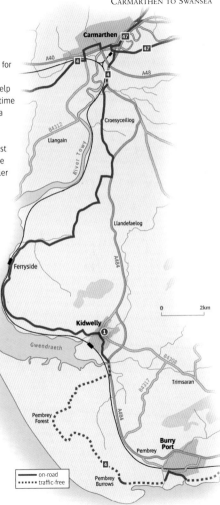

What to see
❶ Kidwelly Castle
Wales may be a country full of castles, but Kidwelly is one of the least-visited and best-preserved links in the chain of strongholds the Normans built along the south coast of Wales. Don't miss it. The most impressive feature is the massive gatehouse.
cadw.wales.gov.uk

◀ Kidwelly Castle

What to see

❶ The National Wetland Centre Give up your saddle for a paddle and spend an hour or two canoeing (April – October) round the wonderful network of lakes and canals that make up this 450-acre wetland wildlife sanctuary, home to a plethora of indigenous and migratory birds. There are also walkways through the saltmarsh, cycle trails and a good café. *wwt.org.uk*

❷ National Waterfront Museum
The remarkable story of the industrial revolution in Wales, told through historical artefacts and the latest interactive technology, housed in an architecturally dramatic building in downtown Swansea. *museumwales.ac.uk/en/swansea*

❸ The Dylan Thomas Centre A permanent exhibition about Thomas' life ('Man and Myth'), as well as a cosy café stuffed with second-hand books. *dylanthomas.com*

ℹ Tourist information centres can be found at the Millennium Coastal Park Visitor Centre, North Dock, Llanelli; Mumbles Road in Mumbles and on Plymouth Street in Swansea.

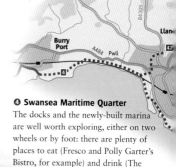

❹ Swansea Maritime Quarter
The docks and the newly-built marina are well worth exploring, either on two wheels or by foot: there are plenty of places to eat (Fresco and Polly Garter's Bistro, for example) and drink (The Queens, near the Waterfront Museum).

Where to stay

You can take your pick from several cheap and cheerful guesthouses and small hotels on Swansea's seafront, but a short detour to The Mumbles, a mile-long strip of pastel-shaded houses, restaurants and pubs at the southern end of Swansea Bay, will give you some better options. **Tides Reach Guest House** (*tidesreachguesthouse.com*),

The Coast House (*thecoasthouse.com*), **Alexandra House** (*alexandra-house.com*) and **Patricks with Rooms** (*patrickswithrooms.com*), are all spic and span guesthouses on Mumbles Road which welcome cyclists.

Spares and repairs

There are several good independent bike shops in Swansea town centre: **Action Bikes** is on St David's Square, **Schmoos of Swansea** is on Wyndham Street, **Wheelies Cycles** is on Uplands Crescent and a little further out in the Enterprise Park at Llansamlet is **Tredz**.

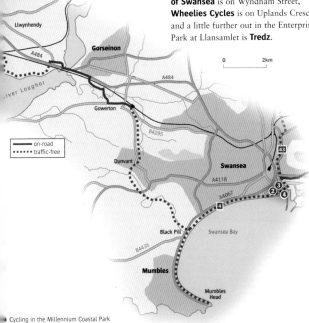

Carmarthen to Swansea
via National Botanic Garden

Distance 72km/45 miles (33km traffic-free) Terrain Only one significant hill; two long, gentle descents on old railway lines; largely on cyclepaths, with one section on a B-road Time 4-5 hours Ascent 460m

An easy section that follows the River Towy east, towards the National Botanic Garden of Wales, before heading south out of the hills to rejoin Route 4 at Llanelli. The two long sections of wonderful, traffic-free cyclepath, from Cross Hands to Loughor Bridge and from Gowerton to Swansea, are largely flat or gently downhill – ideal for families.

From the footbridge over the Towy, head past the railway station and turn right on the main road (A484). At the roundabout, turn right onto Stephens Way and immediately sharp right, cutting back on yourself, under the A484, beside the Towy. Follow this riverside path past Hobbs Bikes (on your right) to meet the B4300. Bear left, following the river east, leaving Carmarthen behind. After 1km, bear left again at the fork, staying on the B4300.

The Towy, your companion for the next 13km, is one of Wales' great rivers: rising

on the soggy moors of the Cambrian Mountains 110km north, it drains over 800 square kilometres of West Wales. The fishing, particularly for sea trout, is renowned. Here, the river coils and twirls lazily across the valley floor, and the B4300 rises and falls gently along the side of the valley to make room.

Approaching Llanarthne, the valley widens: there are wonderful views beyond the village, east to a ruined hilltop castle – an iconic Welsh sight – framed by the glacier-sculpted peaks of the Carmarthen Fans. Paxton's Tower – built to commemorate the death of Lord Nelson at Trafalgar – stands high on the hillside to your right. In Llanarthne, pass the Golden Grove Inn, cross the stream and turn right opposite the Emlyn Arms, heading south up the valley side. After roughly 2.5km of climbing, you reach the rear entrance to the National Botanic Garden of Wales (NBGW): turn left, then right at the gate, to skirt round the perimeter fence to the main entrance.

There's so much to see at NBGW, you could spend days here. But it's worth stopping, even if you only have a couple of hours: see the Great Glasshouse, a spectacular single-span greenhouse and home to some of the world's most endangered plants, or the Apothecaries Garden featuring herbs from around the planet. There are also cafés.

The next 7km to Cefneithin is unspectacular – it's time to put your head down. Follow the B4310, partly on a cyclepath, to Porthyrhyd and turn left just before the T-junction, in front of the Prince of Wales Arms. In Cefneithin, follow the road round to the left and at the bottom of the dip on a long straight, turn right – it's easy to miss. Continue over the stream and a crossroads onto a track: the cyclepath begins in front of the rugby club.

Route 47 follows the disused railway line for 20km, all the way to Llanelli. It's a delightful ride, on tarmac and ever so gently downhill. There are views over the Gwendraeth Fawr Valley, and after Cynheidre you can see the Bristol Channel and the Gower Peninsula. The trail was originally a horse-drawn tramroad, linking the iron furnaces in the valleys with the coast. Authorised by an Act of Parliament in 1802, it may be Britain's first ever public railway operation. Later, the Llanelli and Mynydd Mawr Railway Company transported anthracite down to Llanelli: rail traffic only ceased in 1989, when Cynheidre colliery closed. There are plans to build a heritage centre and make 1km of track operational again.

Below the Lleidi Reservoirs, Route 47 enters the outskirts of Llanelli and the old tramway crosses several roads: take care. Eventually you come to a new footbridge over the A484: cross this to rejoin Route 4

National Botanic Garden

beside the sea in the Millennium Coastal Park. If you're doing a loop back to Carmarthen, turn right here towards Burry Port and Kidwelly; if Swansea is your destination, turn left along the seafront towards the sail-shaped Park Discovery Centre.

There are good cafés at the Discovery Centre (500m from Llanelli train station) and at the Wildfowl and Wetlands Centre (just off the route but worth a detour). The traffic-free section finally, sadly, ends when you cross the railway line and the A484. Via a side street that runs parallel, you return to the A484 to cross the Loughor Bridge. Bear left at the roundabout over the bridge and take the first right on to Pont Y Cob Road which dips back under the railway and along a saltmarsh into Gowerton. For a

highly recommended detour west round the Gower Peninsula – one of Britain's most beautiful protuberances, where Dylan Thomas used to take his "Devils for an airing" – follow the B4295 at the end of Pont Y Cob Road towards Crofty, along the North Gower Trail. To continue on Route 4, turn left and follow the B4295 to Gowerton railway station, then turn right and immediately left on to an old railway line. There is a short diversion from the disused railway through a housing estate – pay attention to the signs – before you start climbing steadily towards Dunvant.

At the Railway Inn, the tarmac path starts to gently descend through the Clyne Valley. At the bottom of this thick broadleaf wood, you abruptly arrive at Black Pill and the busy A4067, on Swansea Bay: turn right

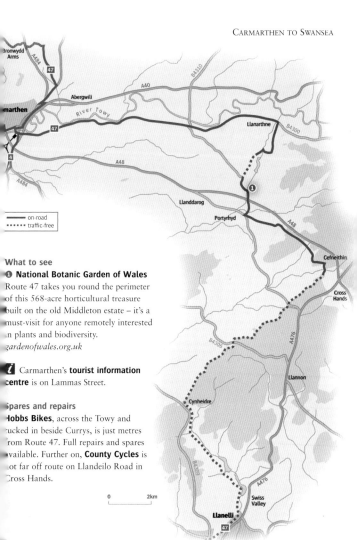

What to see

❶ National Botanic Garden of Wales
Route 47 takes you round the perimeter
of this 568-acre horticultural treasure
built on the old Middleton estate – it's a
must-visit for anyone remotely interested
in plants and biodiversity.
gardenofwales.org.uk

ℹ Carmarthen's **tourist information
centre** is on Lammas Street.

Spares and repairs

Hobbs Bikes, across the Towy and
tucked in beside Currys, is just metres
from Route 47. Full repairs and spares
available. Further on, **County Cycles** is
not far off route on Llandeilo Road in
Cross Hands.

0   2km

◄ On Swansea seafront

51

for the Junction Box Café (50m) and the Victorian seaside resort of Mumbles, once famous for its oyster beds. Turn left along the seafront to Swansea, following the route of the old Mumbles passenger train.

The "ugly, lovely" city, as Dylan Thomas wrote of Swansea, has in recent decades worked hard to slough off its industrial legacy: not easy, since this was the world's leading copper-producing region for over a century. Being flattened during the Blitz in 1941 didn't help Wales' second city, but the Maritime Quarter has been the subject of a major rebuild and is becoming fashionable again.

Route 4 leaves the seafront just before reaching the mouth of the River Tawe: turn left, cross Trawler Road and a footbridge over the marina — it's hard to spot the signs — to reach the Sail Bridge over the River Tawe and the end of this section. Route 43, which will eventually connect Swansea with Brecon and Builth Wells in mid-Wales, meets Route 4 here. The museums, the railway station and the shops are all nearby.

What to see

❶ National Waterfront Museum
The remarkable story of the industrial revolution in Wales, told through historical artefacts and the latest interactive technology, housed in an architecturally dramatic building in downtown Swansea. *museumwales.ac.uk/en/swansea*

❷ Swansea Maritime Quarter The docks and the newly-built marina are well worth exploring, either on two wheels or by foot: there are plenty of places to eat (Fresco and Polly Garter's Bistro, for example) and drink (The Queens, near the Waterfront Museum).

❸ The Dylan Thomas Centre
A permanent exhibition about Thomas' life ('Man and Myth'), as well as a cosy café stuffed with second-hand books.

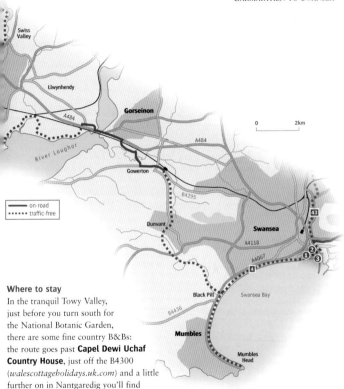

Swiss Valley

Llwynhendy

Gorseinon

A484

A484

River Loughor

Gowerton

B4295

— on-road
••••• traffic-free

Dunvant

Swansea

A4118

A4067

43

①②③

④

Black Pill

Swansea Bay

B4436

Mumbles

Mumbles Head

0   2km

Where to stay

In the tranquil Towy Valley, just before you turn south for the National Botanic Garden, there are some fine country B&Bs: the route goes past **Capel Dewi Uchaf Country House**, just off the B4300 (*walescottageholidays.uk.com*) and a little further on in Nantgaredig you'll find **Ty Castell Guest House** (*ty-castell.co.uk*) and **Dolau Guest House** (*tourlink.co.uk*). Closer to Llanelli at Five Roads, the route passes the welcoming **Waun Wyllt Inn** which has four comfortable rooms in a chalet behind the excellent real-ale serving pub (*waunwyllt.com*). For accommodation in Swansea and Mumbles, see Section 8 (page 47).

Spares and repairs

There are several good independent bike shops in Swansea (see page 47).

i You'll find **tourist information centres** at the Millennium Coastal Park Visitor Centre, North Dock, Llanelli; on Mumbles Road in Mumbles; and on Plymouth Street in Swansea city centre.

◀ Dylan Thomas statue, Swansea

East: Swansea to Chepstow

East of Swansea, the Celtic Trail crosses a quintessential Welsh landscape – the Valleys: the same valleys that poured out coal, iron and sweat to power the Industrial Revolution, as well as poems, hymns, Methodism and Marxism to define the modern nation. To many, this is the heart of Wales.

Today, the collieries are all closed but the network of canals and railway lines, built in the 18th and 19th centuries to transport coal to the coast, remains. Sustrans, in partnership with local authorities, has regenerated lots of these industrial highways and incorporated them into the Celtic Trail: a trip through the Valleys, then, is like a trip through the highlights of our industrial history.

Routes 4 and 47 first split where the Celtic Trail crosses the River Neath,

and rejoin in Pontypridd: the routes could hardly be more different. Route 47 snakes up the Neath Valley before climbing 600m onto forested hilltops and remote moorlands, following a Roman track across the heads of the Rhondda Fawr and Rhondda Fach valleys. It's a long, lonely ride but you're rewarded with superb views over the Carmarthen Fans and the Brecon Beacons to the north, and a memorable descent down forest trails, quiet lanes and an old railway line to reach the River Taff.

Route 4 keeps south, taking in the blustery promenade at Aberavon, the vast Port Talbot Steelworks, the architectural delights of Margam Park and the foothills of the Valleys, to reach Pontypridd.

Routes 4 and 47 split again in Pontypridd. For a few miles, both routes follow the Taff Trail, a long-established Sustrans route from Cardiff to Brecon, via Merthyr Tydfil and the windy heights of the Brecon Beacons. Route 47 leaves the Taff Trail at Quakers Yard to follow a fascinating industrial heritage trail, crossing the Hengoed Viaduct: the highlight is the glorious traffic-free section through Sirhowy Valley Park, though pedalling along the Monmouthshire & Brecon Canal down to Newport is almost as lovely. Both these sections are family-friendly, and with traffic-confident children, they can be connected by a short road section through Crosskeys.

Route 4 takes a more direct route to Newport, leaving the Taff Trail at Nantgarw to take in the magical, concentric castle at Caerphilly before following the River Rhymney. At Newport, the two routes finally become one again for the last, gentle leg across the Gwent Levels to the border town of Chepstow.

Celtic Trail East offers two loop options: from Swansea, over the mountains via Neath to Pontypridd and back via Tondu (125km); and Pontypridd to Newport via the Hengoed Viaduct, returning via Caerphilly (77km). There are several railway stations along Celtic Trail East for anyone who wishes to ride a linear section and return.

Swansea to Tondu

Distance 39km/24.5 miles (25km traffic-free) **Terrain** Largely flat, on cyclepaths, quiet roads and back streets. As Route 4 hugs the coast around Swansea Bay, there's one section beside a major road. There's one short climb into Margam Country Park. A circuit of this park and the leg from Pyle to Tondu or Bridgend (returning by train) would both make excellent family rides **Time** 3 hours 30 **Ascent** 180m

The highlights of this section are Margam Country Park, with its variety of historical attractions, and the lovely traffic-free path through Bedford Park and Parc Slip, two industrial regeneration sites. The first half of the ride snakes through built-up areas and follows busy roads – it's best done at a good lick.

From the Sail Bridge in Swansea, turn left, heading upstream along the River Tawe and right, over the road to reach the A483/Fabian Way. Route 4 runs parallel with and crosses the busy A483: eventually you are forced to join it, on a cyclepath, until you reach the M4. View this first 8km stretch as an opportunity to put your head down. Once under the M4 and over the River Neath, the worst is over. On a cyclepath beside the A48, Routes 4 and 47 split: follow Route 47 north along the canal for Neath and the alternative mountainous route to Pontypridd (see page 64).

Route 4 continues alongside the dual carriageway (A48) on a cyclepath for a further 2.5km: turn right at the roundabout beside Baglan railway station and head southwest through housing estates to Aberavon Sands. With the wind roaring off Swansea Bay and surf dumping onto the beach, it's a glorious 2km traffic-free ride along the seafront. The water may not be an enticing colour but on a hot day, it can be irresistible.

◀ Near Margam House

At the end of the seafront, turn left past the docks and head into Port Talbot, named after the family who built the docks and the famous steelworks. Signs are difficult to follow here: keep the River Afan on your right and, just before you reach the dual carriageway flyover, bear right south of the railway line. At Port Talbot Parkway station (on the Cardiff-Swansea line), go over the level crossing and turn right through the car park. Route 4 heads southeast between the railway line and the A48 for 5km, through back streets, alleys, schoolyards and housing estates. There are signs on lampposts and painted on the tarmac: should you lose these, keep following your nose towards the hills until you hit the cyclepath along the A48 which brings you to a large roundabout over the M4.

Cross the M4 and, on a quiet lane, start climbing gently towards Margam Country Park. With Graig Fawr woodland on your left – a carpet of bluebells in spring – and a stone estate wall on your right, bear left at the fork, uphill. Detour right here to see the impressive Cistercian ruins of Margam Abbey, founded by the illegitimate son of Henry I in 1147, beside the parish church. A little further on, across the lake through the trees, you catch the first glimpses of Margam Castle, a romantic

neo-Gothic extravaganza built by the great Victorian entrepreneur, Christopher Talbot, in the 19th century.

Passing through the estate gates, Route 4 heads north into a wood thick with rhododendrons, round the Iron Age hillfort, Mynydd y Castell, and along the back of the 800-acre deer park, below the gorse-covered hills. There are plenty of reasons to detour into the centre of the park for a few hours – not least, the magnificent Georgian orangery.

Keeping to the high ground, Route 4 leaves the park in the eastern corner by Graig Goch Farm. Turn right on the lane and speed back down to the A48. Turn left and follow the shared-use path beside the A48: this is probably the route of the Roman road through South Wales built by Julius Frontius, who invaded Wales in AD 74-78. After 1.5km, turn left, signposted 'Penybryn', and loop on a quiet lane into the north of Pyle. Cross a stream and turn left under an old railway bridge into a housing estate. After 200m, look for a left turn between two houses along a disused railway line.

Go straight over the roundabout, past the Royal Oak and into Bedford Park, following the route of the old Duffryn, Llynfi & Porthcawl Railway, built to link the ironworks at Maesteg with Porthcawl on the coast. It's a lovely ride through a wood of ash, oak and hawthorn:

CYCLISTS DISMOUNT

BEICWYR MAN DISGYN

in summer, look out for the wildflowers. It's hard to believe this was once an area of hectic industrial activity but the remains of the ironworks at Cefn Cribwr – certainly worth a detour – testify to the time when nature did not prevail.

Turn left on the lane at the end of Bedford Park; go under the railway bridge and right to begin another lovely stretch through a pinewood to Parc Slip Nature Park. Once again, after a century of coal mining, wildlife – including great crested newts, hares, adders and many species of butterfly – has been encouraged back. Various habitats have been created and lapwings, meadow pipits, migratory geese and skylarks are among the bird species you might see. As a stark reminder of what went on here, you pass a monument to the colliery explosion in 1892 that killed 112 men and boys; some survivors were trapped underground for a week.

Route 4 eventually leaves the railway line, crosses a road and drops through a

forest into Tondu where the trail meets the A4063. Turn right, pass under the bridge and turn left along the A4065/Bryn Road – the railway station is to the left. After 200m, cross the river and turn right into a housing estate: a passageway brings you onto the playing fields. This section ends at the millennium signpost beside the Ogmore River, where Routes 4 and 88 meet. Bridgend – with better railway connections and a wider choice of places to stay – is 3km further south, following Route 88.

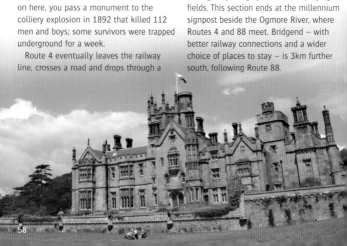

What to see

❶ Margam Country Park Rich in historical importance, Margam Park includes an Iron Age hillfort, a medieval deer park, Tudor gardens, a ruined Cistercian abbey, the neo-Gothic castle, a Georgian orangery and a fine collection of trees and shrubs. There's also loads to entertain the children. *neath-porttalbot.gov.uk/margampark*

❷ Bedford Park Follow the process of iron-making via the interpretive panels at the well-preserved ruins of the Cefn Cribwr Ironworks. There are also the remains of brick works, collieries and mines on the site. *bridgend.gov.uk*

❸ Parc Slip Nature Park Restoration of this opencast mine and colliery coal tip began in the 1980s: today it's made up of plantations, grassland, flower-rich meadows and wetland sites. There's a wealth of wildlife and four bird hides.

❹ Tondu Ironworks The site of the most complete Victorian ironworks in Britain as well as coke ovens, kilns and engine houses.

Where to stay

The functional **Tree Tops Guest House** in Briton Ferry welcomes cyclists (*treetopsguesthouse.com*), as does the **Mountain View B&B Plus** on Talcennau Road in Port Talbot (*mountainview bandbplus.co.uk*) and the **Best Western Aberavon Beach Hotel** (with swimming pool) on the town's seafront (*aberavon beach.com*). Just past Tondu, in Brynmenyn, the welcoming **New Station House B&B** on Bryn Road is also cycle-friendly (*newstationhousebandb.co.uk*).

Spares and repairs

Trailblazer Bikes on Station Road in Port Talbot should have what it takes to get you back on the road. If not, try **H R Cycles** on Five Bells Road in Bridgend.

ℹ The nearest **tourist information centre** is in Bridgend Designer Outlet.

◀ Margam Castle

Tondu to Pontypridd

Distance 22km/14 miles (15km traffic-free) Terrain Largely flat to Blackmill; one climb onto the hillside above Ty'-n-y-bryn, then up and down all the way from Tonyrefail to Pontypridd. A mix of traffic-free paths and quiet lanes. The first section from Tondu to Blackmill along the Ogmore River is a lovely traffic-free ride, ideal for families: it can be extended up Ogmore Vale to Nant-y-moel Time 3 hours Ascent 340m

A short section with a sting in the tail, over the foothills of South Wales through lovely countryside to the hub of the 'Valleys', Pontypridd.

From the millennium signpost on the playing fields in Tondu, where Routes 4 and 88 meet, head northeast along the banks of the Ogmore River. Everyone thinks of Wales as a country of valleys: of course, it's also a country of rivers and the Ogmore is a particularly pretty example. Before the Industrial Revolution, it was a noted salmon river (the Old Welsh word for salmon is 'eog') and with the relatively recent demise of the mines and ironworks along the Ogmore and its tributaries, fishing has improved again.

Save for the odd bit of flood detritus, the river is clean and clear and Route 4 trundles along the bank, through Brynmenyn and

into open countryside. Approaching Blackmill, you pass an ancient oak wood above the meadows. Cross the river at Blackmill and go through the car park, past the café and the Fox and Hounds pub. Cross the main road and, taking care, head down the A4093 for 500m: take the first right, over the Ogmore Fach River and turn left for a delightful 2km section on a rolling lane to a farmhouse. Turn left and right onto a new tarmac, traffic-free path following the disused railway.

Beyond Tynewydd at the end of the traffic-free path, Route 4 continues along the old parish road and then a gravel track, climbing gently onto the hillside with a windfarm whirring away on your right. At the top of this track, in front of a bricked-up farmhouse, go straight ahead onto a lane and drop swiftly down to Thomastown. Turn left at the T-junction and continue north, under the A4093, for 1.5km, to a public park on your right. Follow the perimeter of the park, ducking behind a warehouse and under the A4119, to reach Tonyrefail, an appealing, former mining village of terraced houses that hit hard times when the collieries closed in the 1980s.

Head up the high street – the last place to get something to eat and drink before Pontypridd – and down past the Red Cow, out of town. After 1km of gentle ascent, look for the left turn downhill as the road bends right: it's easy to miss. The last 9km are on quiet lanes, rising and falling along the lower slopes of Mynydd y Glyn. On rural roads like this, it's easy to forget that you're in the Valleys, the most densely populated part of Wales and one of the powerhouses of the Industrial Revolution. A century ago, there were six coalmines within 7km of Pontypridd and the mountains to the north, verdant today, were so discoloured by industry they were known as the 'Black Alps'.

The final descent into Pontypridd is fast and furious. At the roundabout, turn left and follow the cyclepath towards the centre of town, past the rugby ground and beside the river. Pontypridd is situated at the confluence of two rivers, the Taff and the Rhondda, and its importance during the Industrial Revolution was as a transport hub. It is still a good base for exploring the Valleys. Look out for the famous bridge: a 48m single-span, perfect crescent of stone over the Taff. Built by a self-taught mason in 1755, it was a technical miracle and one of the very first signs of the Industrial Revolution arriving in South Wales.

Dismount at the city centre ring road and, following the signs, walk down the pavement to steps which lead to a small side street – lots of cafés and shops – and, via a bridge, to Ynysangharad Park, laid out

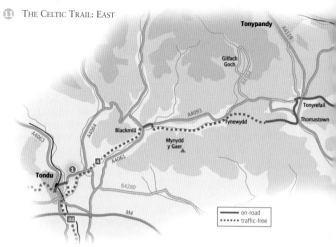

in 1923 by public subscription as a war memorial. There's an exotic statue to honour the father and son team who wrote and composed the Welsh National Anthem, 'Hen Wlad Fy Nhadau' or 'Land of My Fathers'. Turn right over the bridge: this section ends by the signpost in the far corner of the park, on a bend in the River Taff. Route 4 meets the Taff Trail (Route 8) here. Head north on Route 8 if you're either completing a loop back to Swansea (following Route 47 over the mountains – see Section 12, page 64) or if you're following Route 47 to Newport. There are regular trains from Pontypridd to Cardiff, if you're ending a loop-ride here.

What to see

❶ Bryngarw Country Park A short diversion from the cycle route near Brynmenyn takes you to this country house with café, walks and cycle routes.

❷ Pontypridd Museum Housed in a former chapel on Bridge Street, the centre traces the history of the town with displays of agricultural and industrial equipment. Models show the development of the town and there is a working model of the railway station. *pontypriddmuseum.org.uk*

❸ Rhondda Heritage Park A 4km off-road detour from Pontypridd town centre takes you to one of the top heritage visitor attractions in South Wales. Based around the former Lewis Merthyr and Ty Mawr colliery sites at Trehafod, you can find out everything you ever wanted to know about 'Black Gold' and life underground. *rhonddaheritagepark.com*

ℹ There is a **tourist information centre** in the museum on Bridge Street in Pontypridd.

then **The Heritage Park Hotel** is well-positioned right next door to the visitor centre (*heritageparkhotel.co.uk*) and the **Bertie Inn** is just down the road (*thebertie.co.uk*). Heading out of town on Route 47, and handy if you are planning on looping back on the high route to Neath, the comfortable **Tyn-y-Wern Country House** is in the village of Ynysybwl (*tyn-y-wern.co.uk*).

Spares and repairs

Extreme Culture on Bridge Street in Pontypridd has a workshop and carries a good range of spares. You could also make an appointment with **The Bicycle Doctor** in nearby Porth.

Where to stay

There is not a great deal of choice for cyclists in Pontypridd, but if you are planning to take the short off-road detour to Rhondda Heritage Park in Trehafod

Swansea to Pontypridd via Neath (High-level Route)

Distance **64km/40 miles (50km traffic-free)** Terrain Mountainous, largely on forest trails through remote countryside; suitable for mountain bikes only, though you don't need full suspension. You do need to be able to navigate by map and perform all roadside repairs. Carry appropriate clothing and all you need to eat and drink. The section from Briton Ferry to Tonna along the Neath Canal, and the last section, Ynysybwl to Pontypridd, would make excellent family rides Time **7 hours 30** Ascent **800m**

The toughest section of the Celtic Trail with great views of the Brecon Beacons and the Valleys, the route snakes over moorland and through plantations, crossing the mountains that divide the fabled industrial Valleys of South Wales.

Subject to the wind, the section can easily be ridden in the opposite direction to create a loop, connecting with Route 4 through Pontypridd and Swansea, or even as a long, hard day-ride ending in Cardiff or Newport, using the train to return.

From the Sail Bridge in Swansea, turn left, heading upstream along the River Tawe and right, over the road to reach the A483/Fabian Way. Route 4 runs alongside and crosses the busy A483: eventually you are forced to join it, on a cyclepath, as far

as the M4. View this first 8km stretch as an opportunity to put your head down. Once under the M4 and over the River Neath, the worst is over. On a cyclepath beside the A48, Routes 4 and 47 split: follow Route 47 north towards Neath on the west bank of the canal, through the back of an industrial estate.

The towpath, lined with wildflowers, crosses to the other bank for 500m, near Briton Ferry (railway station) and, although it's not especially prepossessing, you are at least away from roads and that Sustrans traffic-free 'karma' is restored. The canal, completed in 1795 when Neath was booming, borders the muddy flats of the river and cuts through the heart of the town, around the back of the railway station.

Though Neath is famed for the coalmines and heavy metal refineries that secured it an important place in industrial history, it's also an ancient town: Route 47 passes the scant remains of the castle (where Edward II briefly took refuge before his grisly death in 1327). One hundred metres further on, beside the canal, is the delightful whitewashed Norman church dedicated to St Illtud, the Celtic warrior-saint who played a large part in the spread of Christianity in Wales.

Continue along the canal, beside the river and the saltmarsh fields, for 1km to the lockhouse at Tonna: cross the canal and climb steeply to the B4434. Turn right and after 1km, turn sharp left uphill, opposite a cemetery: take the opportunity to remove a layer – there's 3km of hefty climbing ahead.

The lane passes between a ruined folly on the prow of a hill and a small reservoir before arriving on the common uplands, covered in coarse grass and sedge vegetation. At a sign exclaiming 'Private Road', go straight on down the track towards the extensive plantations of spruce, fir and larch. The worst of the climb is over, though the route continues to rise gently for several more kilometres.

Turn left at the first crossroads in the forest, and continue on this track, in and out of large clearings, for 4km. Route 47 emerges on to a swath of wild moorland with views north, across the Vale of Neath. Continue to climb towards a stand of wind turbines, looking out for a left turn – it's easy to miss – leading on to a muddy track round the north flanks of the 464m Cefnmawr (Welsh for 'Big ridge'). This track is severely eroded and exposed. It's a push up to the point where you rejoin a well-made forest trail by a millennium signpost by a gate to the windfarm. Around 1km further on, you finally reach the first descent of the day.

These hilltops may be covered in conifer plantations and uninhabited now, but archaeological evidence suggests people lived here from the beginning of the Mesolithic period (10,000BC) until the end of the Bronze Age (1500BC). Certainly the Romans used the ridgeway trail that Route 47 follows to cross the mountains into West Wales.

◄ Hitting the hills from Neath

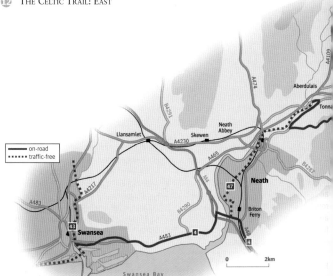

on-road
traffic-free

A4109
A474
Aberdulais
Tonna
B4291
Neath
Abbey
Llansamlet Skewen
A4230
A465
B4291
A4217
M4
B4790
A483 4
A483
43 Swansea
47 **Neath**
Briton
Ferry
A48
4
Swansea Bay

0   2km

Passing the link route to Glyncorrwg on your right, you reach 'Wood Henge', an artwork of constructed wooden poles. At a large fork, bear right and start climbing again. (Left heads downhill and is the link route to Glyn Castle and Resolven.) The aura of peace is punctured at a working quarry in the heart of the forest here – beware the trucks thundering up and down to the A4061. Fork right at the next two junctions and keep climbing – a 2km ascent – to Graig Isaf. At 600m, this is the highest point on the Celtic Trail. There are dramatic views from this craggy cliff edge, over a vast opencast mine in the valley below, towards the heights of the Carmarthen Fans and Pen Y Fan, the highest mountain in South Wales. Just out of sight is Tower Colliery, the oldest-continuously worked deep-coalmine in Britain which was famously bought out by the miners when it faced closure in 1994. After over a decade in profit, the coal finally ran out in 2008 and the mine has closed.

Route 47 descends to cross the A4061 near the top of the great Rhondda-Fawr Valley, perhaps the most famous coal-producing valley in the world and the inspiration for the tune of 'Cwm Rhondda', the unofficial Welsh national anthem. Turn left on the A4061 for 200m – there's a gravel cyclepath – and then right into Beili Glas Forest and enter the Rhondda-Fach Valley ('fawr' and 'fach' are Welsh for 'large

St Illtud's Church, Nea

What to see

❶ Afan Mountain Biking Centre

One of the fastest growing and most exciting mountain biking areas in Britain, Afan Forest Park now has two centres: the newest at Glyncorrwg is only 3km south of Route 47 (follow the signed link route to Glyncorrwg). There's enough tough, highly-technical singletrack to keep enthusiasts sweating for days. *mbwales.com*

and 'small'). There's a lovely descent on a rough gravel track to Lluest-Wen Reservoir and beyond, on tarmac. Look out for the fork 1km below the dam onto a rough track – it's easy to speed past it.

This track rises away from the Rhondda-Fach Valley and drops down to the A4233: turn right along a gravel track and then left – take care crossing the road – before

plunging back into the forest again. The route now follows a ridge heading southeast between the Rhondda-Fach and Cynon Valley to eventually reach the road.

The wild and remote hills are now behind you. Turn left and descend to the picturesque church and the welcoming Brynffynon Arms in Llanwonno.

Turn right below the pub back into the

forest, turn left and climb, before zigzagging down to join the road above Ynysybwl. It's predominantly downhill on a fast lane to Ynysybwl, a town of terraced houses that grew around the site of a colliery founded in the 1880s. Continue through the town and when you're beside the river, look for a sign to the left, to 'Abercynon and Pontypridd'. Cross the river to a disused railway line that idles gently down, alongside the Nant Clydach River. After nearly 3km, leave the traffic-free path at the Cefn Coed bridges and turn right on the road, then right again on a cyclepath that drops underneath the railway line and over the River Taff to meet the Taff Trail beside a rugby ground.

Turn left here, through the cycle gate and round the back of the rugby pitch, if you're

following Route 47 to Newport and don't wish to stop in Pontypridd. If your destination is Pontypridd, turn right and follow the Taff Trail (Route 8) along the river and through back roads into Pontypridd as far as Ynysangharad Park, where this section ends on a bend in the Taff beside the centre of town. Route 47 rejoins Route 4 here. There are regular trains from Pontypridd to Cardiff, if you're ending a loop-ride.

❶ Llanwonno Church Dedicated to and probably founded by St Gwonno, one of the great company of Celtic Saints who spread Christianity in Wales, this delightful parish church sits precariously on a hillside. The church itself was rebuilt in the Gothic style in 1894, but the atmospheric churchyard, with wonderful views down the valley, hints at the 1400 years of unbroken Christian worship on this site.

ℹ There is a **tourist information centre** a short distance off-route at Aberdulais Falls near Tonna, and at Bridge Street in Pontypridd.

Where to stay

Just 3km off-route after you pass the windfarm, the **Glyncorrwg Mountain Bike Centre**, as well as being the trailhead for some great singletrack runs, has a campsite with showers, café and bike shop nearby (*forestry.gov.uk*). Back down in the valley, **Tyn-y-Wern Country House** (*tyn-y-wern.co.uk*) awaits in the village of Ynysybwl. For other accommodation in Pontypridd, see Section 11 (page 63).

Spares and repairs

Skyline Cycles at the Glyncorrwg Mountain Bike Centre (3km off route) will help you out and **Extreme Culture** on Bridge Street in Pontypridd also has a well-stocked workshop.

69

Pontypridd to Newport via Caerphilly

Distance 35km/22 miles (26km traffic-free) Terrain Flat or gently undulating, on a mix of cyclepaths and quiet country lanes. Two notable climbs between Machen and Bassaleg in the Rhymney Valley. No family-friendly sections Time 2-3 hours Ascent 370m

The heart of this ride is along the River Rhymney, which you follow by riverside path, railway line and quiet lanes from the outskirts of Caerphilly almost to the suburbs of Newport. It's worth paying close attention to Route 4 signs from Bassaleg and through Newport as ongoing improvements may result in changes to the route.

From the signpost in the corner of Ynysangharad Park in Pontypridd, follow Routes 4 and 8 (the Taff Trail) along the River Taff to a footbridge over the A470. Turn right down Pentrebach Road (A4054) and left at the junction towards Glyntaff Cemetery. Curiously, the origin of modern cremation is found in Pontypridd. The eccentric Dr William Price, a self-proclaimed druid and naturist, was arrested in 1884 for cremating his son. The ensuing court case led to the legalisation of cremation in Britain in 1902.

Just before the church, look for a right turn which skirts round the south side of the cemetery and leads onto a wooded cyclepath which keeps to the high ground: the only reminder that you're in the industrialised heartland of the Taff Vale is

the drone of the main road below. After 5km, this trail ends: turn right and skirt round to meet the A468 at Nantgarw, where the highly-prized porcelain was made briefly in the early 19th century. Taking care, cross the main road and drop down into the woods to meet a disused railway line. Turn right along the Taff Trail if you're bound for Cardiff (13km). Go left, gently uphill on Route 4, for Caerphilly.

After 1km, leave the railway line and cross the A469 into the colourless outskirts of Caerphilly. Route 4 winds through housing estates, down towards the centre of town. Pay attention to the signs on lampposts and on the tarmac – there are many turns and it's easy to get lost. Eventually, you catch the first glimpse of the mighty turrets and arrive at the park encircling the castle grounds.

This medieval fortress, the first concentrically built castle in Britain, is a

magnificent site: with a cock-eyed tower, it's like something from a child's imagination or a grand sandcastle moments before being engulfed by the tide. Construction dates from 1268 – turbulent times for the Anglo-Norman hegemony in South Wales. Route 4 skirts the moat round to the main gatehouse.

Drop down Castle Street and, crossing over the junction, head away from the castle down Brynau Road. Turn left and then right, leading to a swathe of green park: cross the stream and continue east until you reach the ring road. Taking care, turn left, following a cyclepath and, after 400m, right. This cyclepath leads to a lane: go past the Fisherman's Rest pub, cross the River Rhymney and turn right on to the lovely riverside path.

After 2km, the trail hits the A468: cross over and climb up through a wooded valley to meet the route of a disused colliery railway between Trethomas and Machen: turn right beside the restored signal posts. At the end of the track, just past the Forge and Hammer Inn, drop down steeply into Machen, crossing the A468 and the River

▼ Caerphilly Castle

Rhymney again.
A steep climb on a
tranquil single-track lane
brings you back into the
Rhymney Valley: it's a fine
undulating ride down the west bank of
the river through pretty farmland dotted
with stands of broadleaf woodland. In fact,
the valley feels a little like the Welsh Home
Counties, with ostentatious gates and
intercom systems fronting the large, well-
tended houses.

In Draethen, turn left in front of the Holly
Bush Inn. After a further 3km, cross the river
and turn left to begin a 1.5km climb. The
reward comes swiftly in the form of a long
descent into Bassaleg. Turn right down a
lane and left past the school to reach the
A468. Head straight on at the roundabout
beside the Tredegar Arms and cross the dual
carriageway (A467) on a footbridge. Follow
the pavement/cyclepath down the east side
of the A467 until you reach a gap in the
wall: head left across a piece of open
heathland and through a tunnel under the
M4 onto the Tredegar Park playing fields.
At the end of the playing fields, dismount
and cross the B4237, then follow the
cyclepath along the dual carriageway (A48),
over the Ebbw River. The route forks away
from the main road, over a railway line and
down a street of warehouse-size shops.
Eventually, you catch a glimpse of the

strange lattice-work pillars of the
Transporter Bridge – your goal.

Newport, Wales' third largest city, grew
up around the docks at the mouth of the
River Usk, just south of Route 4 and the
A48. In the city's mid-19th century heyday,
seven million tons of coal were exported a
year. The centre of town and railway station
are now 2km north. There you'll find all
shops and amenities, as well as the
Westgate Hotel, the front entrance of which
still bears the bullet holes from the Chartist
Uprising in 1839, calling for universal male
suffrage. You can find out the full story at
the excellent Museum and Art Gallery.

This section rejoins Route 47 for the final
time, and ends at the Victorian Transporter
Bridge, built in 1906 by Ferdinand Arnodin,
the father of transporter bridges, to bear
people and horses across the Usk without
interrupting high-masted ships on the river.
The 'gondola' – a sort of aerial ferry – can
carry up to six cars: bicycles cross for free.

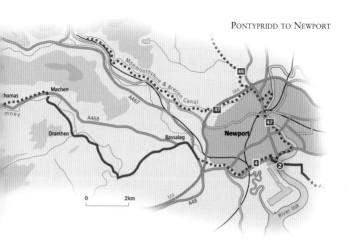

What to see

① Caerphilly Castle Built between 1268 and 1271 by the powerful English lord Gilbert de Clare, imposing Caerphilly is one of the UK's great medieval castles with an unmatched series of concentric fortifications. The walls were never tested in battle, however, and the leaning southeast corner was the victim of subsidence, not cannon. *caerphillycastle.com*

② Newport Transporter Bridge Spanning the River Usk, the towers of this Grade 1-listed structure stand 196m apart and rise 74m above road level. Electrically powered, the gondola is pulled by a cable wound round a drum in the motorhouse on the east bank at a maximum speed of 3m per second. *fontb.org.uk*

ⓘ There is a **tourist information centre** opposite the castle in Caerphilly and on John Frost Square in Newport.

Where to stay

There are plenty of good functional B&Bs in and around Newport, including **St Etienne** and **The Knoll** on Stow Hill and **Annesley House** and **Ashburton House** on Caerleon Road (*newport.gov.uk*), but if you want something just a little bit different – daleks, telephone boxes, flotation tanks – then head for the eccentric **West Usk Lighthouse** at St Brides to the south of town. The sea views from the quirky wedge-shaped rooms of this Grade 2-listed former lighthouse are worth the detour (*westusklighthouse.co.uk*). Leaving Newport, the tranquil ivy-clad **Brick House Country Guest House** in Redwick also welcomes cyclists.

Spares and repairs

Abercycles & Accessories on the High Street in Caerphilly or **R G Callow Cycles** on Caerleon Road in Newport will help you out.

Pontypridd to Newport via Hengoed Viaduct

Distance 42km/26 miles (36km traffic-free)
Terrain Almost entirely on traffic-free
paths. After a gentle climb with one short,
steep section to Treharris, it's nearly all
flat or downhill to Newport: in short, one
long, glorious family-friendly section
Time 3-4 hours Ascent 220m

**A superb ride which strings together
railway paths, canals and new
cyclepaths through several excellent
land-regeneration projects that have
transformed the post-industrialised
Valleys of South Wales.**

From Ynysangharad Park in Pontypridd,
follow the Taff Trail (Route 8) north out of
town on minor roads and then along the
cyclepath beside the River Taff. At
Cilfynydd, 4km north of Pontypridd, Route
47 heads west across the river and over the
mountains to Swansea via Neath (see
Section 12, page 64). If you have come
from Swansea and you're following Route

47 without detouring to Pontypridd, continue along Route 8 and Route 47, through the cycle gate and around the rugby pitch, north to Abercynon.

The River Taff, as a fishery, has almost gone full circle: before the Industrial Revolution, it was a noted salmon and trout river. Through its tributaries, it drains many of the coal-mining valleys of South Wales and for over a century, sewage, chemicals and hot cinders from the ironworks were dumped in it. It's said it used to run black with coal-dust. Not surprisingly, it became highly polluted and uninhabited by fish. Today, as you can see breezing along the cyclepath, the river is much cleaner again and, happily, the fish have returned.

After another 2.5km, the riverside cyclepath ends on a lane in front of a row of old cottages: turn left and left again on the main road in front of the Navigation pub. After 100m, turn right down a lane beside a small fire station onto Tram Road Side – one of those classic Sustrans routes that swiftly remove you from the cacophony of the main roads. You're now following the route of the Penydarren Tramroad, scene of the first ever steam locomotive journey in 1804. A decade before George Stephenson, Richard Trevithick's engine pulled ten tons of iron and 70 passengers from Merthyr to the canal head at Abercynon.

Cross the Taff on the old stone tramroad

bridge into Quakers Yard. Routes 8 and 47 split here: the Taff Trail goes straight on, towards Merthyr Tydfil; Route 47 goes right, over the river and across a main road (A4054). Immediately, turn left down Mill Street, next to the Quakers Yard Inn and opposite the Bridge Stores.

After 100m, look for the turning over a footbridge and climb steeply up the zigzags to the village of Treharris, named after Harris, the investor who opened the famous colliery here in 1878 ('Tre' is Welsh for town or home): the mine closed in 1991. Follow Route 47 across the new single-span footbridge over the Cascades of the Taff Bargoed River (it's confusing, there are three Taff rivers) and through an arch onto a cyclepath along Trelewis high street. This leads to a bridge over an operational mineral railway line: turn right and follow the tracks through the bottom of Parc Penallta Country Park.

Parc Penallta, between Hengoed and Nelson, is on the site of the last working deep mine in the Rhymney Valley: it's one of a string of excellent regeneration projects on former colliery sites that are attracting wildlife and visitors back to the Valleys. It's well worth diverting off Route 47 through the park.

Route 47 goes under one and across two

'The Wheel of Drams' by Hengoed Viaduct

By the Monmouthshire and Brecon Canal ▸

roads, then round the Hengoed Community Centre to reach the great Hengoed Viaduct. This 260m high, 16-arch, listed viaduct over the Rhymney Valley was built in 1857 to complete the rail route linking all the valleys between Pontypool and Swansea: it's a staggering feat of engineering and the 'Wheel of Drams' – an 8m-high sculpture built from steel coal drams in the shape of a wheel – was commissioned to commemorate the transfer of use from railway to cyclepath.

Follow the old railway line through Maesycwmmer to meet the A472 and follow this busy dual carriageway, on a cyclepath, downhill to the Sirhowy Valley where one of the most delightful sections of the entire Celtic Trail – perfect for families – begins. Leave the A472 and

follow a lane down to a gravel cyclepath and the beginning of the disused tramroad which descends, almost imperceptibly, through this steeply-sided valley. The soundtrack to this ride is the river churning over the rocks below: it is thought the name of the valley may derive from the Welsh for 'wild or angry water' – 'sorwy'.

After seven blissful kilometres, go through a car park and look for the left turn by a stone cottage that leads down to and over the river. A road brings you to Crosskeys: cross another, smaller river and immediately turn right into Waunfawr Park. In the opposite corner of the park, cross over into Blackvein Road, turn right at the T-junction and first left, round the back of a cemetery, taking care crossing the Ebbw Vale to Cardiff railway line and up to the

Crumlin branch of the old Monmouthshire and Brecon Canal. Turn right for a glorious ride – 12km of flat or downhill on the towpath – all the way to Newport. There's a pub – Prince of Wales – on your right after 1.5km, as the canal bends left round the mountain.

As with the viaducts and the tram-roads, the canal was also built when the Welsh Valleys emerged as the powerhouse of the Industrial Revolution: the Canal Navigation Act of 1792 authorised its construction to connect the great ironworks at the heads of the Valleys with the docks in Newport. When it fell into disrepair in the early 20th century, numerous roads were built over it: take care crossing these. At the top of Fourteen Locks, where the canal centre has been rebuilt, the towpath hares off downhill. Pass under

the M4 and turn left along the canal to Newport, keeping an eye out for the brilliant blue dash of kingfishers.

Route 47 leaves the canal at Barrack Hill near the city centre. At a major road intersection, take the footbridge over one main road and, looking carefully for the signs, pass under a flyover to reach a park beside the River Usk. Turn right along the tidal river. Just past Sainsbury's, you come to the 14th-century ruin of Newport Castle. Newport railway station is 200m from the castle, towards the centre of town. Continue along the river, on a cyclepath and then alongside the busy A4042, to reach the Transporter Bridge, where this section ends, and Route 47 reconnects with Route 4 for the final time.

◂ On Hengoed Viaduct

Newport Transporter Bridge ▶

What to see

❶ Parc Penallta Country Park The main attractions of this 180-hectare regeneration project require a short diversion from Route 47: the collection of public artworks include 'Sultan, the Pit Pony' – a vast landscape sculpture – and the 360-degree views from the High Point Observatory are superb. *caerphilly.gov.uk*

❸ Fourteen Locks Canal Centre Find out all about the Monmouthshire Canal and the remarkable flight of 14 locks which raise the water level 50m in a distance of 740m at the recently refurbished centre. You can also get a refreshing cuppa in the Dadford Tea Room. *fourteenlocks.co.uk*

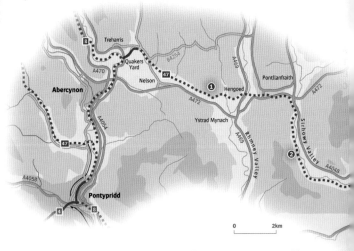

❷ Sirhowy Valley Park There are several worthwhile diversions – the Flatwoods Meadows Nature Reserve and Graig Goch Woods are both glorious in spring. *caerphilly.gov.uk/countryside*

❹ Newport Transporter Bridge Spanning the River Usk, the towers of this Grade 1-listed structure stand 196m apart and rise 74m above road level. Electrically powered, the gondola is pulled by a cable wound round a drum in the motorhouse on the east bank at a maximum speed of 3m per second. *fontb.org.uk*

ℹ There is a **tourist information centre** on John Frost Square in Newport.

Where to stay

A short detour from the route at Treharris takes you to the **E2 Welsh International Climbing and Activity Centre** where you can stay the night in comfortable bunkhouse-style accommodation and give climbing, bouldering or caving a try if you want a break from the saddle (*e2-adventures.com*).

Further on, near Hengoed, **Highfields** at Tir-y-Berth Farm offers cycle-friendly bed and breakfast (*visitcaerphilly.com*). For accommodation in Newport, see Section 13 (page 73).

Spares and repairs

Martin Ashfield Cycles on St Mary's Street in Risca and **R G Callow Cycles** on Caerleon Road in Newport will help you out.

79

Newport to Chepstow

Distance 37km/23 miles (8km traffic-free)
Terrain Predominantly flat on quiet country lanes across the Gwent Levels, with one steep climb up to Chepstow. Newport to Severn Tunnel Junction Station would make a good family ride for traffic-confident children – mainly lanes with a bit of cyclepath – returning by train
Time 2-3 hours **Ascent** 180m

The dominant geographical feature of this, the last and easiest section of the Celtic Trail, is the Severn Estuary – the largest coastal plain estuary in the UK with the second largest tidal range in the world. The Gwent Levels are made up of land reclaimed from it and there are regular glimpses of the great, brown expanse of water and the two bridges that span its width.

If, when you make your journey, the Victorian Transporter Bridge is still closed for structural repairs, follow the A48 upstream along the shared-use pavement on the riverside. After 1km, cross the Usk on City Bridge and at the first traffic lights, turn right to head back downstream, parallel with the river. There's a cyclepath along the pavement; after 1.5km, where the road turns right under a tunnel, cut left onto a cinder track which winds away from Newport's industrial suburbs, under electricity pylons, across a grazing marsh. If the Transporter Bridge is open, simply cross this, turn right at the end of the road and follow the cyclepath to the tunnel.

The track ends by a millennium signpost at Pye Corner. Go straight across at the junction on to a quiet lane. Almost immediately you're among the rectangular

fields, pollarded willows and stagnant, brackish drainage ditches (called 'reens' in Wales) that are the hallmarks of this open, fen-like landscape. At the next junction, by a stone bridge over a reen, turn left. At the end of a 1.5km arrow-straight road, with the massive Llanwern Steel Works on your left, turn right at the small crossroads, signposted 'Redwick'.

The process of land reclamation began in Roman times, but the majority of the reen system – built primarily to drain the fields into the sea during the wettest months of the year – dates from the medieval period or later. On the green in the pretty village of Redwick, there is an old water control station containing some ancient drainage artefacts. Of course, the great threat to a man-made reclaimed environment like this is flooding: scratched on the south porch of the church of St Thomas the Apostle in Redwick is a mark showing the height the water reached during the notorious flood of 1607, one of the greatest natural disasters ever to hit Britain. The Gwent Levels were completely submerged and Redwick was under 2m of water.

The medieval stocks are still in situ beside the graveyard: more welcoming is the Rose Inn, opposite. If you're not in a hurry, Redwick is a lovely place to idle for a while: it's 500m southeast from the village to the muddy banks of the Severn Estuary.

Route 4 continues northeast, parallel with the estuary, past several quaint stone cottages, to Undy. Turn right at a small crossroads just as you come into the village, and right again as you leave it. At the end of the lane, turn left and go down a rough gravel track marked 'Private Road'. After 150m, follow the track to the right, and then after 750m, take the left turn. There are plenty of potholes but the track is perfectly rideable on a hybrid. There are views of the modern Severn Bridge. After another 1.25km, you meet tarmac again: turn left and cross over the M4.

Almost immediately turn right (Severn Tunnel Junction railway station – trains to Bristol and Newport – is 250m straight ahead) and follow the small tarmac road 1.5km to Caldicot railway station (trains to Gloucester and Newport). Route 4 goes under the railway line and into the centre of Caldicot – divert here to visit the Norman fortress on the west of town or continue north through a housing estate and under the M48.

Now you've left the Gwent Levels behind, there's more traffic and the route starts to roll gently up and down. Turn right at the junction in Caerwent: the Romans built the market town of Venta Silurum in 75AD and the ruins of large sections of the Roman town walls, the basilica, the temple and various other buildings are still visible in this quiet village: it's worth exploring.

At the A48, turn right and follow the cyclepath alongside this busy road to Crick: turn left just before the M48, signposted 'Shirenewton' and, after 100m, right onto a small lane shadowing the motorway

◀ Chepstow Castle

through a pretty vale. Go left at the fork and right at the T-junction, to reach the brow of a hill with views towards the old Severn Bridge. Left at the next T-junction and right at the fork brings you down into a hidden valley and the picturesque village of Mounton. Turn right at the mini-roundabout and brace yourself for the last ascent of the Celtic Trail. If you've ridden the whole of it, this climb may prompt less than sweet remembrances of hills past, in the Preselis, perhaps, or on the Pembrokeshire coast, beside the Towy Estuary or above the Neath Valley. It's 1.25km up to meet the A466: turn right on the cyclepath alongside the A466, then turn left, eventually reaching a one-way street to the centre of Chepstow.

The high street runs parallel with the busy A48. Keep going down, through the Town Gate, until you hit Bridge Street.

The Celtic Trail ends in an appropriately beautiful and historic spot: beside the tranquil River Wye, beneath the towering limestone walls of Chepstow Castle. If your journey also ends here, the railway station is behind the supermarket, across the A48. Of course, this may just be the end of the beginning of your journey. Chepstow has been a crossroads for centuries and the spider's web of Sustrans routes leads in all directions from here: Route 42 heads northeast to Gloucester, via the Forest of Dean, and northwest to Hay via the Wye Valley and the Black Mountains.

A cyclepath across the old Severn Bridge opens up the whole of southern England: you can follow Route 4 all the way to London or take Route 3 down to Devon and Cornwall. Wales may be behind you, but the rest of the British Isles lies ahead.

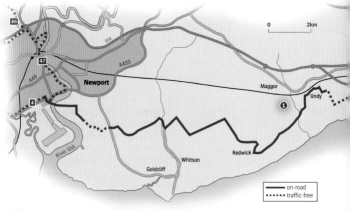

on-road
traffic-free

What to see

❶ Gwent Levels Wildlife Trust manages several reserves close to Route 4. Magor Marsh Reserve is the last remnant of traditional fenland: in spring, the meadows are full of rare wildflowers, and many wetland bird species inhabit the ponds. *gwentwildlife.org*

❷ Caldicot Castle The ruins of this significant medieval stronghold are now used for a multitude of events from Civil War battle re-enactments to medieval pageants: if you've cycled with the family from Newport, spend the afternoon here and return by train. *caldicotcastle.co.uk*

❸ Caerwent Known to the Romans as Venta Silurum, Caerwent was the site of the main settlement of the defeated Silures tribe. The foundations of a 4th-century Roman temple and several other buildings and walls are visible.

❹ Chepstow Museum This award-winning museum, in a delightful townhouse opposite the castle, tells the fascinating story of Chepstow – fortified outpost, port, market town and early tourist attraction – through the centuries.

❺ Chepstow Castle Begun in 1067 by William FitzOsbern, one of the great Marcher Lords appointed by William the Conqueror to secure the borderlands (the first castle built by the Normans west of Offa's Dyke), it was strategically important for centuries. It's fascinating inside; the greatest aspect is from the river, above which the castle walls rise like a limestone tower.

Where to stay

For fans of real ale, the **Coach and Horses Inn** on Welsh Street overlooking Chepstow Castle is the place to enjoy beer, bed and breakfast (*thecoachandhorsesinn.co.uk*). Also near the castle, on Bridge Street, you will find the historic **Castle View Hotel** (*hotelchepstow.co.uk*) and restaurant with rooms, **Afon Gwy** (*afongwy.co.uk*).

Spares and repairs

You'll find the excellent **559 Bikes** on Manor Way in Chepstow town centre.

There is a **tourist information centre** on Bridge Street, near the castle, in Chepstow.

Taff Trail detour

Distance **89km/55 miles (56km traffic-free)** Terrain **Mostly tarmac cyclepaths; best for hybrid or hardtail mountain bikes; one early climb followed by a long, gentle descent if starting from Brecon. Family-friendly sections between Merthyr Tydfil and Cardiff for children confident enough to cross busy roads** Time **9 hours** Ascent **560m**

Both Routes 4 and 47 of the Celtic Trail interlink with and follow sections of Wales's longest-established cycle route, the Taff Trail (Route 8). If you have a day or two to spare, however, you can detour to ride the entire length of it.

Starting in the delightful market town of Brecon, the Taff Trail scales the windy heights of the Brecon Beacons and descends through the Taff Vale via Merthyr Tydfil and Pontypridd to reach the Cardiff docks, a legacy of the great Victorian export boom. The trail is 89km (55 miles) long. For the greater part, it follows traffic-free, tarmac cyclepaths which you'll speed along: at a push, it can be ridden in a day, but allowing two provides time to take in the rich industrial heritage and the glorious natural landscapes.

The trail can be ridden in either direction, though my slight preference (and the direction it's described here) is to ride from

Brecon

A40

Llanfrynach

River Usk

on-road
traffic-free

Talybont-on-Usk

Brecon Beacons

Talybont Reservoir

Pentwyn Reservoir

Pontsticill Reservoir

0   3km

①

A465

Merthyr Tydfil

②

A4060

A470

north to south: this way, you get the one big climb (from the Usk Valley to the high point of the trail in the Brecon Beacons) out of the way early on; the rest of the route largely comprises a gentle descent, dropping 215m over 48km alongside the River Taff, into the heart of the capital. (Of course, if you're heading north on Route 8/Lôn Las Cymru into mid-Wales, you'll be riding south to north.)

Hybrid or hardtail mountain bikes, probably with semi-slick tyres, are ideal for the Taff Trail. Between Merthyr Tydfil and Cardiff, the trail is family-friendly, though children must be at least confident enough to cross over busy roads. If they are, then it's a great route for kids, partly because of the gentle incline, but also because the cyclepaths follow a mix of disused tramways, railways, canals and viaducts that steer away from the roads and are often wide enough to ride two abreast.

From Brecon, the Taff Trail heads east along the leafy Monmouthshire and Brecon Canal as far as Llanfrynach. Near Talybont-on-Usk, it takes to the hills — there are two alternative routes for the ascent, but either

What to see

① Brecon Mountain Railway For a more leisurely view of the Brecon Beacons, you can't beat taking the steam locomotive from Pant Station to the north end of Taf Fechan Reservoir and back. *breconmountainrailway.co.uk*

② Cyfarthfa Castle This grand castellated mansion was built in 1824 by the 'Ironmaster' William Crawshay who made his fortune from the ironworks it looked down on. The basement houses a museum dedicated to Merthyr's turbulent history.

◀ Cefn Coed Viaduct

way, it's a long slog up onto the moorland beneath the glacial-sculpted cirques of the Brecon Beacons. A swift descent through Taf Fechan Forest brings you alongside Pontsticill Reservoir before you join a lovely old railway line that drops into Merthyr Tydfil, once the largest iron-producing town in the world.

Here you leave behind the open countryside and the captivating industrial history of the iron and coal industries takes its place. You cross the Cefn Coed Viaduct and pass the Cyfarthfa Ironworks (site of the first blast furnace in 1765), rows of workers' cottages and the town of Aberfan to reach Quakers Yard. Route 8 meets Route 47 here – see Sections 13 and 14 (pages 70-79) for details of the route as far as Nantgarw.

South of Nantgarw, the Taff Trail drops through woodland on a disused railway line to the 'fairytale castle', Castell Coch. Approaching the outskirts of Cardiff, the route returns to the River Taff which you follow through Llandaff and Bute Park, past the Millennium Stadium and the railway station, to reach the recently redeveloped docks area.

Between the end of May and the end of September, Beacons Bus runs a Sunday service with a bike trailer between Cardiff and Brecon: if you can organise your detour to start or finish on a Sunday, this service

i There is a **tourist information centre** by the main car park in Brecon, on Glebeland Street next to the bus station in Merthyr Tydfil and on Bridge Street in Pontypridd. In Cardiff, head for The Tube on Harbour Drive.

0	3km

— on-road
····· traffic-free

(breconbeacons.org) might facilitate your trip. You could, for example, follow the Celtic Trail to Pontypridd, then detour on the Taff Trail down to Cardiff, take the bus to Brecon and then follow the Taff Trail again, via Merthyr Tydfil, as far as Quakers Yard, to rejoin the Celtic Trail.

The Millennium Centre in Cardiff ▶

What to see

❶ Castell Coch The 'Red Castle' near Tongwynlais was built during the 1870s on the foundations of an earlier medieval structure as a country retreat for the very wealthy 3rd Marquess of Bute. The 'fairytale' castle is also home to a good café on the ground floor.

❷ Cardiff Castle Although the site has been fortified for over 2000 years, the castle as it is today is largely the work of the 3rd Marquess of Bute and his architect William Burges. Indulging his fascination with astrology, religious symbolism and Gothic architecture, the Marquess created a stunning fantasy world within the castle walls. *cardiffcastle.com*

❸ Cardiff Bay Visitor Centre Known locally as 'The Tube', this oval structure houses a large-scale model of the Bay and through its exhibitions tells the story of the regeneration of the docklands. *cardiff.gov.uk*

Where to stay

Pretty much everything a tired cyclist could want can be found at **The Bridge Café** on Brecon's Bridge Street (*bridgecafe.co.uk*). The **Brecon (Ty'n-y-Caeau) Youth Hostel** (*yha.org.uk*) is also very convenient, just off the trail at Groesffordd. En route, Merthyr is home to a number of B&Bs but you may want to push on to Treharris and the **E2 Welsh International Climbing and Activity Centre** (*e2-adventures.com*). In Cardiff, the **Youth Hostel** near Roath Park is the city's best budget option (*yha.org.uk*).

Spares and repairs

In Brecon, **Bi-Ped Cycles** on Ship Street has a workshop and helpful staff. **Taff Vale Cycles**, near the Cyfarthfa Retail Park in Merthyr Tydfil and **Extreme Culture** on Bridge Street in Pontypridd will also keep you on the road. In Cardiff, **The Bike Shed** on Wyndham Crescent, **Cyclopaedia** on Crwys Road and **Sunset Mountain Bikes** on Woodville Road are all within easy reach of the trail.

YMUNWCH Â'R MUDIAD

sustrans

JOIN THE MOVEMENT

━━━ National Cycle Network

Holyhead
Llandudno
Prestatyn
Chester
Caernarfon
Snowdonia National Park
Shrewsbury
Tywyn
Machynlleth
Aberystwyth
Llanidloes
Cardigan
Lampeter
Builth Wells
Hay-on-Wye
Hereford
Fishguard
St Davids
Pembrokeshire Coast National Park
Carmarthen
Brecon Beacons National Park
Ystradgynlais
Brynmawr
Abergavenny
Pembroke
Tenby
Merthyr Tydfil
Chepstow
Pontypridd
Newport
Swansea
Bridgend
Cardiff

© Crown Copyright. Sustrans 2008